CIMA

INTEGRATED CASE STUDY

PRACTICE
WORKBOOK

MANAGEMENT LEVEL

FOR EXAMS FROM NOV 2015 TO NOV 2016

Second edition September 2015

ISBN 9781 4727 4294 0
e-ISBN 9781 4727 4297 1

British Library Cataloguing-in-Publication Data
A catalogue record for this book
is available from the British Library

Published by

BPP Learning Media Ltd
BPP House, Aldine Place, 142/144 Uxbridge Road
London W12 8AA

www.bpp.com/learningmedia

Printed in the United Kingdom by

Ricoh UK Limited
Unit 2
Wells Place
Merstham
RH1 3LG

Your learning materials, published by BPP Learning
Media Ltd, are printed on paper obtained from
traceable, sustainable sources.

BPP
LEARNING MEDIA

Contents

Topic 1 - Welcome to the Integrated Case Study

1 Welcome to the Integrated Case Study

What role does the ICS exam play in the 2015 Syllabus?

It complements the Objective Test exams – having demonstrated their detailed technical competence in the OT exams, the ICS exam enables CIMA to ensure students can put their theoretical understanding to use in a real world situation.

The ICS exam enables CIMA to assess important competencies like the ability to communicate appropriately and consider impacts of decisions across a whole business.

It contributes to CIMA's aim of producing competent and confident management accountants – in passing the ICS exams, students show that they can perform well in real world situations.

What's the ICS exam format, and how does it differ from the Objective Test exams?

They are very different, and this means you need to prepare in a different way:

Objective Test Exam	Integrated Case Study Exam
Per paper	Per Level
Computer-based	Computer-based
1.5 hours	3 hours
Auto-marked	Human-marked
On Demand	Quarterly sittings
Immediate results	4-5 week turnaround
All component learning outcomes	High-level themes from each paper
Short OTQs	Long-form "Tasks"
Technical/theoretical focus	Competency/application in the real world focus
70% pass mark	60% pass mark (equivalent of scaled score 80+)
No requirement to pass individual syllabus areas	Also need to achieve minimum threshold (approx 1/3 of marks available) per relevant competency

What role will the student play?

In the exam you will be asked to take on a role, and this varies in seniority depending on the level of the qualification. Here's CIMA's official guidance:

	Operational	Management	Strategic
Job role	Finance officer	Manager	Senior manager
Audience – who you are seeking to influence	Your manager/peers, product owners	CFO, FD, senior business managers – may be non financial	CFO/Board, senior management team – may be non financial
Technical skills	Core accounting and finance skills such as preparing budgets and costings; financial statements. Advice on product decisions such as mix, volume, price and short term funding; identifying stakeholders.	Preparing plans for final reporting including group accounts for a number of entities. Analyse and manage costs using information produced at operational level. Ensure compliance with tax and regulatory regimes.	Analysis of strategic options, including options for funding, risk management and reporting. Formulating financial strategy.
Business skills	Understanding the role of finance in the business and regulatory environment. Gathering finance and non financial information for decision making.	Defining short term goals. Understanding the environment in which the business operates, identifying stakeholders, appreciation of risk.	Understanding the implications of strategic decisions for the future of the business, its markets, stakeholders and competitors. Identifying the best course for future developments, including financing.
People skills	Communicating with peers and non finance staff to put together or advise others on budgets.	Communicating plans in order to influence or empower as an aid to decision making.	Advanced communication for stakeholders to understand the implications and value of plans; influencing, collaborating and negotiating with stakeholders. Advanced decision making.
Leadership skills	Enthusing and empowering colleagues through clear communication.	Managing change, driving performance improvements.	Effective change management, empowering and leading teams. Motivating and inspiring performance.

How will the ICS exam span the three pillars?

The three pillars of the CIMA Syllabus are there for a reason. They are the different dimensions a business must consider to be successful. The relationship between these will be reflected in your ICS exam.

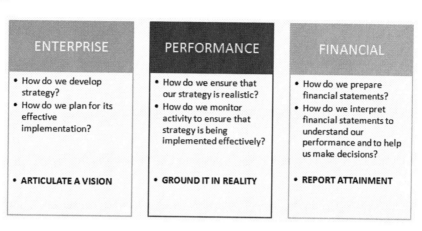

ENTERPRISE	PERFORMANCE	FINANCIAL
• How do we develop strategy? • How do we plan for its effective implementation?	• How do we ensure that our strategy is realistic? • How do we monitor activity to ensure that strategy is being implemented effectively?	• How do we prepare financial statements? • How do we interpret financial statements to understand our performance and to help us make decisions?
• ARTICULATE A VISION	• GROUND IT IN REALITY	• REPORT ATTAINMENT

What will happen in the ICS exam?

- You will be given access to the preseen case study information 6/7 weeks before your exam

- The exam will simulate 3 hours in your role (see above) for the company in the preseen

- You will be presented with Tasks to complete, usually in the form of an email from your line manager

- You will be provided with other "unseen" information as the exam progresses, and you will need to quickly assimilate this with what you already know from the preseen.

- You will need to type in your responses to the Tasks set, usually in the form of an email response to your line manager

- Tasks are timed (usually 30min – 1hr each), and you will be automatically moved on to the next Task when the timer counts down to zero

- You cannot go back to a previous Task when the timer has reached zero

- You can 'skip' to the next Task whenever you wish, but you do not bank any time – ie your total exam time will now be less than three hours

What therefore are the key elements of an ICS exam?

Exam Technique	Time management will be very important in the ICS exam, as will your ability to quickly identify what is being asked for in a Task and structuring your answer accordingly
ICS exam environment	Becoming familiar with working in the ICS exam environment will be a great benefit in preparing for the exam
Core competencies	The Tasks in the exam and the syllabus areas they focus on will give you the opportunity to demonstrate your competence in Core Accounting Skills, Business Acumen, People Skills and Leadership Skills
Integration	You will be expected to move smoothly between the pillars, and provide coherent answers that consider all perspectives
Real preseen	You need to understand the real case study sufficiently such that you can place yourself in this world in the real exam, and therefore ensure everything you type relates entirely to the case study organisation. You will effectively be working for a different company for three hours in your exam!
Technical Knowledge	It is very important to remember that you have already demonstrated your detailed technical competence in passing the exams (or being exempt) for the individual papers in the level. The ICS exam will not test you again on the finest detail of the technical theory, instead it will check you can demonstrate how a management accountant adds value to a business in very practical terms in the real world.

How can I study effectively for my ICS exam?

Do

✓ Produce a study plan. The study window for the ICS exam is pretty condensed so you need to ensure you have a study plan that works for you.

✓ Try to think in an ICS way when you're back at work e.g. "what are the impacts of the business deciding to do X?", "how well was Y communicated?", "if I structure my emails like this, will my line manager be able to understand me more clearly?"

✓ Absorb any business news you can – anything from new product launches, to acquisitions and change management issues, big share price changes and legal cases – try to imagine the management accountants involvement in any of these back in the business where it is all happening. Where should they be adding value?

✓ Practice as many Tasks as you can. There are lots in this Workbook! Make sure you learn something from every Task you attempt – having a consistent approach to 'self review' is a good way of doing this, and we'll return to that later.

Do NOT

× Allow yourself to get dragged back into all of the technical detail of the individual syllabus content for each paper in the Level. It's the key themes and topics that you need to have with you for your ICS preparations, and "the factors that need to be considered" in a practical sense when a business is considering applying the theory in the real world.

× Become too obsessed nor spend huge amounts of time trying to memorise every last bit of information provided in the real preseen case study. Whilst you need to be 'very familiar' with the real preseen in time for your exam, you must not go too far with this to the point where it detracts from the amount of Task practice you are doing to develop your exam skills.

× Try to do everything all at once, or try to remember everything at once from across the whole level. There's too much! You should just focus on one practice Task at a time during your preparations, gradually building up to full mock exams as the real exam draws near.

BPP
LEARNING MEDIA

Topic 2 - Getting up to speed

2 Getting up to speed

Overview

To get to this stage in your studies you have already demonstrated to CIMA that you have the required level of competence in terms of the detailed technical content in the syllabus for each of the three papers in the level.

To allow you to focus on developing the specific skills and competencies you need to be successful in the ICS exam, it makes sense to ensure you are 'up to speed' as soon as possible.

This means ensuring you are still familiar with the key topic areas and themes from your studies of each individual paper, and this Topic will help you to structure how you do this.

Once you are 'up to speed' you can then turn your attention to the all important ICS Task Practice, and to bringing the real preseen case study into your preparations.

Technical Content from the individual papers

There are two aspects to this. The first is a general one – basically, can you remember the key learning points and main themes from your earlier studies of each paper? The second is a more specific one – what do you need to look at to ensure you have covered the new topics that have come in to the syllabus as part of the CIMA 2015 syllabus update if you studied any of the individual papers under the old syllabus?

1.   Refreshing high-level understanding from Objective Test papers

In preparing for your ICS exam through attempting Practice Tasks (see Topics 4, 5 and 6) it will be helpful to ensure you can remember the <u>key themes</u> from the syllabus content for each individual paper in the Level.

With the exception of brand new syllabus topics (see 2. below) you should keep your 'OT refresh' at a high-level, and avoid going back into the detail required for an OT exam.

2.   2015 Syllabus changes – what this means for your ICS exam

Given that the 2015 Syllabus update has seen some brand new topics enter the Management Level syllabus, and some topics move between papers so they are now viewed from a different perspective, you need something more than a 'refresher' to ensure you are up to speed for your ICS studies.

The information below will clarify for you what is new, or significantly changed, within the 2015 Management Level, and guide you as to where you will be able to find learning content to help you fill any knowledge gaps in a targeted and efficient way.

Where <u>significant knowledge gaps caused by the transition</u> do need to be filled, that is, on topics you haven't studied in the 2010 Syllabus, you may find that a more detailed approach is necessary to properly develop your understanding of the key themes you need for your ICS studies.

The information below will help you with this.

E2

E2 has been updated to include a clearer focus on the role of the CGMA in managing an enterprise. This is reflected in the greater emphasis on managing relations between the finance department and other stakeholders, as well as how to undertake environmental and competitor analysis. To make way for the new material the syllabus section on Project Management has been significantly streamlined.

IN	Reference to 2015 BPP Course Notes
Achieving sustainable competitive advantage	Chapter 1a Section 12
Behavioural aspects of management accounting	Chapter 7 Section 2
The importance of organisational culture	Chapter 5
Managing relationships between the finance team and a range of internal and external stakeholders	Chapter 7 Section 4
Managing organisational change, and recommend how to manage resistance to change	Chapter 8
Environmental and competitor analysis (from E1)	Chapter 3 Section 1 & 2
Collection and interpretation of trend data (from E1)	Chapter 3 Section 5
Discuss HRM aspects of managing and controlling individuals' performance	Chapter 6 Section 7

OUT
Tools and techniques of project management

P2

The revisions to the P2 syllabus reflect a greater emphasis on the long-term outcomes of financial decision making. This is seen in the inclusion of more investment appraisal and risk management theory, at the expense of more short-term decision making frameworks such as linear programming and 'what If' scenarios.

IN	Reference to 2015 BPP Course Notes
Analysing risk and uncertainty – Bayes Theorem	Chapter 10 section 2
Discussing risk management via TARA framework, business risks, ethical implications and the public interest	Chapter 10 section 3
Risks arising from information – Big Data	Chapter 10 section 4
Identification and integration of non-financial factors in long-term decisions	Chapter 8 section 1
Analyse information for use in long-term decision making (from P1)	Chapter 8 section 1
Discuss the financial consequences of dealing with long-run projects (from P1)	Chapters 8 and 9
Evaluate investment appraisal techniques and explain their results (from P1)	Chapters 8 and 9
Apply sensitivity analysis (from P1)	Chapter 10 section 1
Analyse risk and uncertainty (from P1)	Chapter 10 section 1
Real options (from F3)	Chapter 9 section 3
Modified internal rate of return (from F3)	Chapter 8 section 3
Costs and benefits of IT investments (from F3)	Chapter 10 section 4

OUT
Relevant cashflows and their use in short term decisions
Limiting factors and linear programming
Fixed & flexible budget report

F2

This paper has been broadened, and amended to create clearer links through to the F3 paper. The new content covers some accounting standards that were previously in F1, and some content such as long-term finance that was previously in F3. These additions have been balanced by the removal of some entire topics such as substance over form, reconstructions and external reporting.

IN	Reference to 2015 BPP Course Notes
Characteristics of different types of long-term debt and equity finance	Chapter 1 Sections 1 - 2
Markets and methods for raising long-term finance	Chapter 1 Sections 3 - 4
Calculating cost of equity via dividend valuation model - ke	Chapter 2 Section 2
Calculating post-tax cost of debt - kd	Chapter 2 Sections 3 - 6
Calculating the weighted average cost of capital - WACC	Chapter 2 Section 7
IASs/IFRSs on revenue, leases, provisions, deferred taxation and construction contracts (from F1), and the associated accounting entries for these	Chapter 4 Leases Chapter 5 Provisions Chapter 6 Deferred taxation Chapter 8 Revenue and construction contracts
Ethical selection of accounting policies and estimates	Chapter 18
Disclosure of related party transactions	Chapter 16
Advice on improving financial performance and financial position	Chapter 19 Section 5

OUT
Groups – foreign transactions (foreign subsidiaries are still examinable), capital reconstruction schemes, demergers, associate to subsidiary step acquisitions
Recognition and measurement – substance over form, hedge accounting (IAS 39), financial instruments' disclosures (IFRS 7), employee benefits (IAS 19), asset valuation and changing prices, fair value measurement (IFRS 13)
Analysis and interpretation – segment reporting (IFRS 8)
External reporting

Topic 3 – Preparing to pass

BPP
LEARNING MEDIA

3 Preparing to pass

Core Competencies

Overview

The old-fashioned stereotype of an accountant is someone who is excellent at number-crunching but hopeless at interacting with others. If the accountancy profession really was like this, its members would be unable to compete with the processing power of a computer and become extinct.

CIMA's new syllabus emphasises that, while understanding accounting concepts is crucial to being an accountant, this skill must be exercised in conjunction with other skills if it is to be of real value in the modern business environment. Following comprehensive global research with organisations of various sizes in different sectors, CIMA have developed a framework which shows the skills, abilities and competencies that finance professionals need to help drive the success of their organisations.

The competency framework is based on what today's organisations **expect finance professionals to do**: -

- Perform accounting and finance activities within the context of the business

- Influence the decisions, actions and behaviours of their colleagues

- Provide leadership at all levels

To do this successfully, finance professionals need core accounting and finance skills, business acumen, people skills and leadership skills.

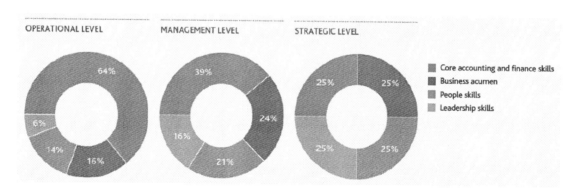

These competencies are underpinned by **ethics**, **integrity** and **professionalism**.

What does this mean for the exam?

In practical terms it means you need to **treat the 3 hours of the exam as if you were an employee of the case study organisation**. You need to respond to the exam Tasks as if they were requests from your **real** line manager in **your** real job. The exam is designed to replicate the workplace, as opposed to asking students to provide answers to abstract academic questions.

The good news here is that you have been developing these skills through your life in general and your workplace in particular. The more that you can bring this real life experience into your ICS exam, the more marks you are likely to score. In fact, **the ICS format should naturally incline you to demonstrate these skills**.

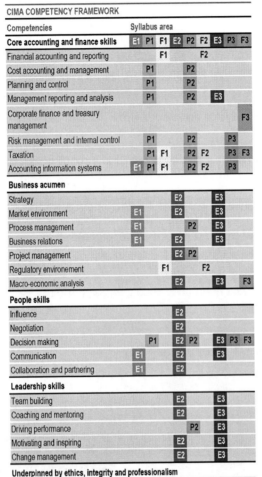

It means that the marks you score for answering questions will be spread across the four competencies, and in passing the exam you are therefore demonstrating you have the skill set that today's organisations require and that you can use what you have learned to make a difference in the workplace.

CIMA have provided the mapping table (opposite) that indicates how the competencies identified in their consultation with employers fit into the overall framework.

In the ICS exam this indicates that the marks you are awarded for Tasks primarily set in the P- or F-pillars will be allocated to the core accounting and finance skills competency in the main, with some in business acumen.

Marks you are awarded for predominantly E-pillar Tasks will be allocated to the business acumen, people skills and leadership skills activities.

In summary, to score good marks in the ICS exam you need to:

- Select the correct techniques and principles to use for the task in hand and demonstrate that you understand them properly (**core accounting and finance skills**)

- You need to so in the context of the scenario as if you worked for the organisation in the question, drawing on the preseen information where relevant (**business skills**)

- You need to identify the human impacts of management accounting and tailor your responses to Tasks to the recipient to show that you can communicate effectively (**people skills**)

- You need to make recommendations on the benefits of taking a particular course of action and how it can be best implemented (**leadership**)

Core Accounting and Finance Skills (39%)

The thing that makes accountants unique is their ability to use a range of financial and accounting tools. These cover financial accounting and reporting, cost accounting and management, planning and control, management reporting and analysis, corporate finance and treasure management, risk management and internal control, taxation and accounting information systems.

To demonstrate competence in this area, it is not enough to understand these concepts and be able to use them. You will also need to be able to use your discretion to determine which tool is the most appropriate in a given situation and discuss its relative advantages / disadvantages.

Remember – when you give advice to a manager or client, they're not interested in how much you know or how many theories you can mention – all they want is an answer to their problem!

At Management Level, the exam marks allocated to the technical skills competency are likely to come from SubTasks set within the P2 and/or F2 syllabus.

Business Acumen (24%)

Commercially valuable advice needs to be tailored to the organisation and environment. While CIMA does not expect any specialist knowledge of real-life political or environmental conditions, you will be expected to demonstrate that you can tailor your advice to a unique environment.

This advice is likely to relate to strategic decision-making, analysis of market and macro-economic environments, process management, business relations, project management and awareness of the regulatory environment.

This competency requires you to review the technical advice you are about to give and consider whether it is realistic given the organisation's condition. For example, there is no point in recommending an expansion strategy to an organisation with no capital operating in a declining market!

At Management Level, the exam marks allocated to the business skills competency are likely to come from SubTasks set within the E-pillar syllabus.

People Skills (21%)

As an accountant, you will be one of many stakeholders in an organisation who contribute to its overall direction. The other stakeholders are unlikely to understand the complexities of the accountancy solutions you are proposing, so you may need to demystify the technical content depending on your audience. You will certainly have to communicate clearly and engagingly.

You also need to recognise the human impacts of management accounting and ensure these are taken into account in business decisions.

At Management Level, the exam marks allocated to the people skills competency are likely to come from SubTasks set within the E-pillar syllabus. That said, any SubTasks that require you to explain something technical to a non-financial recipient could also be allocated to this competency as a test of your communication skills.

Leadership Skills (16%)

The advice that accountants give has implications across the whole organisation and beyond. It is therefore crucial for the accountant to demonstrate leadership if a proposed course of action is to be converted into a meaningful result.

Leadership can take many forms, but will include team-building, coaching and mentoring, driving performance, managing change, and an ability to motivate and inspire. It can include recommending improvements and persuading others of the benefits of following your proposals. It can also be identifying what is required to move things forward and managing implementation.

At Management Level, the exam marks allocated to the leadership skills competency are likely to come from E-pillar based SubTasks.

A note on integration

There are a small number of integration marks that can be awarded in the exam (approximately 6 marks at Management Level). There are various ways that these can be picked up in your answers to Tasks, for example by:

1. Bringing in points from another pillar (compared to the pillar in which a Task or SubTask is predominantly set.

2. Bringing in points from another competency (eg suggesting how an issue could be best communicated to stakeholders even though not specifically asked to do this in the requirement)

3. Using an appropriate communication style for the audience

4. Making specific reference to info in the preseen

5. Including practical illustrations of points

6. Providing thorough/comprehensive answers (ie answering all parts of a Task in a logical and cohesive way)

Exam Technique

Overview

Excellent exam technique ensures you maximise your marks in the real exam. It means you score the most marks you can given your level of understanding of the syllabus content by the time you reach the real exam.

The style and format of the Integrated Case Study exam means that **your exam technique will be more important than ever**.

What is it about the ICS exam that makes exam technique so important?

- The ICS exam assumes you have already demonstrated your competence in terms of technical knowledge, so the focus shifts to showing you can deal with "finance professional" tasks in a real world situation

- All the Tasks are timed in the exam so you simply do not have the option of taking longer to produce your answer than the exam timings allow

- You are not allowed to return to your previous answers to make any changes once the timer has moved on to the next Task

- Although you can move on to the next Task before the timer has counted down to zero, you are not allowed to 'bank' any time you didn't use, you will simply have an exam that lasts less than three hours in total.

- All of your answers have to relate to the case study and be directly applicable to the case study organisation. You have to approach the exam as if you are employed by them, and live in their world.

- You need to ensure you are interpreting the task correctly and doing what is expected by your line manager or whoever is giving you the Task to do.

- If you miss out a SubTask altogether you risk failing the exam as you may have missed a chunk of marks that related to a single competency.

- In order to do all of this really well, planning your answer will be as critical as ever!

So, what does 'excellent ICS exam technique' consist of?

It can be captured nicely in our TIPS approach:

> **T**ime management at Task level
> **I**dentifying the requirement
> **P**lanning your answer in context
> **S**peaking to your audience

We'll now look at these in more detail.

Time Management at Task Level

The ICS exam is three hours long, and made up of a number of individually timed Tasks. Your challenge is to be able to produce a good quality response to the task set **within the timings for each individual task**. It is likely the 'average' ICS exam will look like this:

	Duration of each Task	Total number of Tasks
Strategic Level	60 mins	3
Management Level	30 – 60 mins	4
Operational Level	35 – 55 mins	4

In this time you need to:

1. Identify exactly what is required of you
2. Efficiently digest the information provided in the Task
3. Plan your answer
4. Produce your answer

It is vital that for every Task/SubTask in the exam that you get to the point where you have at least produced a good and complete response in the time allowed. You need to do so without taking any shortcuts in preceding stages, or else you risk your whole answer diverging from the point and failing to respond to the specific requirements of the Task.

You should practice these elements in turn, gradually bringing them together in full Task practice, so that you speed up and find you can hit exam timings come the big day.

Identifying the Requirement

Unlike the traditional way in which exam questions are presented where the exact requirement is very clearly provided AFTER the question/scenario, in 2015 ICS tasks this will be different:

- Exactly what you need to do may well be spread throughout an email from your manager (eg different 'subtasks' flagged up in different paragraphs of the email) as opposed to the traditional approach of them all being in one place with a helpful box around them.

- Depending on how specifically the task is worded, you may need to exercise some professional judgement as to how to respond, just as you would in the real world. Exactly what is required of you is likely to be pretty clear at Operational Level – but less so as you reach Strategic Level, as the issues faced become more complex.

The word "and"

The individual requirements in a Task may seem pretty straightforward to spot if they are presented to you as a bulleted list or in separate sentences, but even then you MUST look for the word 'and' within a requirement as this implies there's more than one thing you need to do and that the marking scheme will reflect this. If you miss what comes after the 'and' you may only be able to score half marks at most.

It is very important that you clearly identify what is required before moving on to the 'Planning' stage. With sufficient practice you will find you can do this with increased confidence and speed.

Planning your answer in context

Having identified what is required, you now need to plan how you are going to respond.

The **recommended approach** is to do this "onscreen" – ie as if you were typing the outline for an email before running through and adding all the detail in afterwards. This is more time efficient than using the Pearson Vue wipeboard (approx 10 sides of laminated white paper) provided to you in the exam with a wipe-able pen.

A key part of your planning is to consider how much time you have to do the Task and to split this time between any SubTasks. You need to decide what the key points are that you want to make in your response, and how many points to make / how much detail to go into.

When planning you MUST specifically focus on the <u>**situation facing the company in the question**</u>, such that when you produce your answer in full it relates as much as it can to the scenario.

An **important aspect** here is to avoid spending too long producing a very detailed plan that gives you too much to do in the time. Just like in the real world, you will need to limit your communications to the most relevant/important/salient points. Equally, you need to include enough coverage to provide the 'value' that the organisation needs in order to take positive action. This will come with practice and feedback as you prepare for your real exam.

Speaking to your Audience

You will be expected to demonstrate that you can tailor the way you communicate when responding to Tasks, based on the recipient of your response. There are some overlaps here with the People Skills competency, in that CIMA (and employers) want their finance professionals to be able to communicate effectively with the full range of stakeholders in a business.

Marks can and will be awarded in the exam for evidence of 'appropriate communication'

When you are producing your full answer, the main aspect to consider here is whether the recipient has a financial background. If not, then you should look to provide a more fundamental explanation of any of the relevant techniques or concepts in such a way that will help them to understand your main points better.

At Strategic Level, you may be expected to consider the varying perspectives and agendas of different stakeholders and to take this into account in how you construct your response.

As you work through practice Tasks, ensure you think about "how can I phrase my response to make sure the recipient best understands my key points?"

Let's now bring this all together in to our **recommended approach** for the full ICS exam…

ICS Exam – the best practical approach

Here's a very practical and efficient 10-step approach to working your way through each Task in a full 3 hour ICS exam:

60 mins	33 marks
55 mins	31 marks
50 mins	28 marks
45 mins	25 marks
40 mins	22 marks
35 mins	19 marks

1. Note how many **minutes you have to complete the Task** and the amount of marks this implies the Task is worth. Approximately: -

2. Skip forward (using the 'Next' button) until you reach the screen where the **requirements are given for the Task**.

3. Make sure you **identify them all** and **calculate the split** of time/marks between each SubTask.

4. Use what you are being asked to do in each SubTask **as a subheading and type it in** to your answer space – this is the structure the marker will be looking for.

5. Now go back and **read the unseen info** you are provided with as part of the Task. Given you know what the requirements are you now know what you are looking for as you read through.

6. Make sure that you also consider "What is relevant in the **preseen** here?"

7. As you are reading, **insert bullet points beneath your subheadings** of the points that you want to make. As a sensible rule of thumb you should aim for 2 marks per point, so use this to calculate how many bullets you need beneath each subheading

8. When you have populated your onscreen plan in the answer box, you can now return to the first SubTask and start to **turn your points into full sentences**, remembering your role and who the recipient is.

9. You are working for the real preseen company! You must make sure you **relate your answer to the company/industry** as much as possible.

10. Keep an **eye on the time for the Task** as it ticks down. You MUST manage your time within a Task to ensure you give a **good response to each SubTask**. If you miss the last one out as you run out of time then you've just missed out on a sizable number of marks of the 100 available, and potentially a large proportion of those available for an individual competency.

Self Review – How to Guide

Guidance

How do you know you're doing well at work? You wouldn't send a random email to your manager, forget about it and then wait for them to tell you what they thought of it. You'd review your own work very carefully before sending it. You will get the very most out of your Task Practice if you apply the same principles of self-review, especially if you do so in a consistent and structured way.

The role and importance of effective Self-Review

- Will enable you to continually learn as you go

- You need to be effective and efficient in how you study and the way to do this is through adopting the best study habits of which structured self-review is right at the top

- Your answer will never match the suggested solution provided for a variety of reasons, so a line by line comparison is unlikely to yield any useful insight.

- The most important thing here is that you think back on **how you got to the answer**, and whether any problems crept in at an **early stage** – eg on reflection you misinterpreted the requirement or didn't plan properly. The reason this is so important is that improving your approach here will lead to more **marks in the exam for any and every Task!**

- Reviewing your answer **and how you approached it** in a systematic way will help you to focus on specific aspects that you can consciously look to improve next time. This is much more effective than just thinking "must try harder" or "my answer needs to be more like the suggested solution"

The <u>Self-Review Template</u> provided on the following pages is a good framework for doing this

- Print or photocopy yourself further blank versions of this and use it whenever you practice a Task

- Do your initial review **BEFORE** you look at the suggested solution. Take a step back and ask yourself "how happy am I with what I've produced here?"

- Don't feel obliged to note something in every box for every Task. We'd recommend that capturing 2-3 improvement points is enough for any single Task

- Keep them with you (perhaps inserted in this Workbook) so you can refer back whenever you need to

- In due course you're likely to have more than one attempt at some Practice Tasks – looking at your completed Template from the first time will be a great way of reminding you what you need to focus on during your second attempt (and then you could update your Template with your second review)

Integrated Case Study Tasks – Self Review	Practice Task Ref:
	What did I do well and what will I do even better next time?
Time Management	
Identifying the Requirement	
Planning my answer	
Ensuring set within the scenario/preseen	
Speaking to the audience	
Key syllabus areas	
Other review comments	

Integrated Case Study Tasks – Self Review	Practice Task Ref:
	What did I do well and what will I do even better next time?
Time Management	
Identifying the Requirement	
Planning my answer	
Ensuring set within the scenario/preseen	
Speaking to the audience	
Key syllabus areas	
Other review comments	

Integrated Case Study Tasks – Self Review	Practice Task Ref:
	What did I do well and what will I do even better next time?
Time Management	
Identifying the Requirement	
Planning my answer	
Ensuring set within the scenario/preseen	
Speaking to the audience	
Key syllabus areas	
Other review comments	

Integrated Case Study Tasks – Self Review	Practice Task Ref:
	What did I do well and what will I do even better next time?
Time Management	
Identifying the Requirement	
Planning my answer	
Ensuring set within the scenario/preseen	
Speaking to the audience	
Key syllabus areas	
Other review comments	

Integrated Case Study Tasks – Self Review	Practice Task Ref:
	What did I do well and what will I do even better next time?
Time Management	
Identifying the Requirement	
Planning my answer	
Ensuring set within the scenario/preseen	
Speaking to the audience	
Key syllabus areas	
Other review comments	

Integrated Case Study Tasks – Self Review	Practice Task Ref:
	What did I do well and what will I do even better next time?
Time Management	
Identifying the Requirement	
Planning my answer	
Ensuring set within the scenario/preseen	
Speaking to the audience	
Key syllabus areas	
Other review comments	

Topic 4 – P2 Task Practice

The Practice Tasks that follow are intended to serve several purposes:

- They are spread across the key topics in the syllabus, to enable you to recap important areas of technical knowledge

- Although not based on the real preseen they have been designed to reflect the style of the Tasks in the ICS Exam, so that you can use them to develop your ICS Exam Technique

- Note that as they are not based on a separate preseen, they contain more background/scenario information than you would expect in the 'unseen' Tasks in your real exam.

- The solutions are intended to be "student achievable" and reflective of the level of detail CIMA provide in their Examiners Solutions.

- They should provide you with a good range of business situations that could be applied to the real preseen. As well as attempting each Practice Task in its own right, you should also take some to reflect afterwards as to how the issues you've worked through could relate to the real preseen organisation.

Topic 4 – P2 Primary Tasks

Task 1 - ZZ

(indicative timing excluding background information : 45 mins)

Background information

You are Tom Smart, employed as a management accountant at ZZ Co. ZZ manufactures and sells electronic personal grooming and beauty products. The products are sold throughout the world and 90% of ZZ's total revenue comes from export sales. The production takes place in one factory. Materials are sourced from a variety of suppliers.

ZZ is not dominant in the markets in which it operates and, as a result, it has to accept the market price for each of its products.

Today is 4th June 20X5.

You have just received the following extract from the board meeting minutes from 15th May 20X5

ZZ

Meeting Minutes

15th May 20X5

Next meeting: 15th June 20X5

Falling margins

The Managing Director stated that the company is now coming under increasing pressure from competitors and is he is increasingly concerned about falling margins. He stated that it is essential to earn a satisfactory profit at each stage throughout a product's life cycle.

The Managing Director discussed the need to build a reputation for quality especially as ZZ gives a five year guarantee with all of its products. He asked all Board members to consider potential ways of reducing costs and increasing profits whilst enhancing quality.

Subsequent to the Board meeting held on 15th May 20X5, Mr Watts, the Financial Director, sends you the following e-mail:

From: Andrew Watts AW@ZZ.co.uk

To: Tom Smart TS@ZZ.co.uk

Sent: 17th May 20X5, 10.04 a.m.

Subject: Falling margins

Tom,

I have been asked to consider potential ways of reducing costs and increasing profits and would like some ideas from you.

As you know, ZZ prepares annual budgets and sets a standard cost for each different product at the start of each year. Variance reports are produced every month.

It would be very useful for me if you could prepare us a report which covers the following:

- How ZZ could use target costing and kaizen costing to improve its future performance, including an explanation of the differences between target costing and kaizen costing

- How ZZ can use standard costing and variance analysis to prepare meaningful reports when using kaizen costing-

- How ZZ could analyse its costs of quality and reduce them

Many thanks,

Andrew

Andrew Watts

Financial Director

ZZ

E: AW@ZZ.co.uk

T: 0117 900100

Write your response to the email from Andrew

Task 2 - PT

(indicative timing excluding background information : 45 mins)

Background information

PT is a small manufacturer of consumer electronic goods. PT constantly develops new products that are in high demand as they use the latest technology and are 'must haves' for consumers who want to own the latest gadgets. Many of its products have a life cycle of one year or less.

You are Sophie Best, recently employed as a management accountant by PT.

Task

Today is 7th June 20X5

The Marketing Director has sent you the following email.

From:	Rachel Fisher RF@PT.co.uk
To:	Sophie Best SB@PT.co.uk
Sent:	7th June 20X5, 10.04 a.m.

Subject: Pricing strategies

Sophie,

Welcome to PT!

Your predecessor helped to formulate the pricing strategies for our products and I need some help understanding them. Different pricing strategies were used for Products R, Q and S (see Exhibit 1) and I'm hoping that you will be able to explain some of the issues for me.

- What is the difference between penetration and skimming pricing strategies?

- What usually happens to unit selling prices and unit production costs in the growth and maturity stages of the product life cycle?

- What are the disadvantages of 'total cost plus' pricing, and

- Are there any disadvantages to setting a price based on profit maximisation using demand forecasts?

Kind regards,

Rachel

Rachel Fisher

Marketing Director

RDF

Exhibit 1

Product pricing

Product R	Product Q	Product S
Innovative and unique	Launched last year	Launched last year
Launched at a market skimming high price last month	Life cycle expected to be 2 years	Life cycle expected to be 5 years
Life cycle expected to be 1 year	Price based on costs plus a 10% profit margin	Price based on profit maximisation using demand forecasts
	Losing market share rapidly	

Write your response to the email from Rachel.

Task 3 - CW

(indicative timing excluding background information - 45 mins)

Background information

CW is a retail company that operates five stores. Each store has a manager and there is also a General Manager, Pippa Parker who reports directly to the Board of Directors of the company.

For many years the General Manager has set the budgets for each store and the store managers' performances have been measured against their respective budgets even though they did not actively participate in their preparation. If a store manager meets his budgeted target then he is financially rewarded for his performance.

The company has recently appointed a new Finance Director, George Grant, who has questioned this previous practice and suggested that changes should be made to the budgeting process at CW. George has suggested that each store manager should be involved in the preparation of their own budget and that CW should follow the principles of 'Beyond Budgeting'.

Task

Today is 4th June 20X5.

You are Helen Black, employed as a management accountant at CW Co.

George has emailed the following extract from academic research to Pippa Parker.

Exhibit 1

In an age of discontinuous change, unpredictable competition and fickle customers, few companies can plan ahead with any confidence – yet most organisations remain locked into a 'plan-make-and-sell' business model that involves a protracted annual budgeting process based on negotiated targets and that assumes customers will buy what the company decides to make. Such assumptions are no longer valid in an age when customers can switch loyalties at the click of a mouse.

J Hope and R Fraser *Beyond Budgeting (Strategic Finance 10/2000)*

You have just received the following email from Pippa Parker asking you to be part of a working party.

From:	Pippa Parker PP@CW.co.uk
To:	Helen Black HB@CW.co.uk
Sent:	4th June 20X5, 10.04 a.m.

Subject: Budgets

Helen,

I would like you to be part of a working party that has been established to consider ways to improve the budgeting process at CW.

Before the first meeting I would like you to prepare some notes that cover the following issues:

- The problems that could arise, for planning and decision making purposes within CW, if the store managers overstated their budgeted costs and resource requirements.

- The behavioural issues that could arise if excess costs and resources are removed from the store managers' budgets.

- How the principles of "Beyond Budgeting" promote a cultural framework that could be suitable for CW.

Write your response to the email from Pippa

Task 4 - HTL

(indicative timing excl. background information - email 1 : 25 mins, email 2 : 25 mins)

Background information

You are Lee Ridley, employed as a management accountant at HTL. HTL owns three hotels in different regions of the same country. The company uses the same accounting policies and cost of capital of 10% per annum for all the hotels that it owns. All rooms are sold on a 'bed and breakfast' basis. The hotels are open for 365 days per year. The restaurants provide breakfasts to hotel guests only. At all other times the restaurants are available to hotel guests and the general public.

The manager of a hotel receives an annual bonus if the hotel's Return on Net Assets is maintained or improved.

Today is 8th January 20X2

You have recently submitted a summary of financial information for each hotel for the year ended 31 December 20X1 to the Managing Director, Phil Webster.

Exhibit 1

Hotel	Northern	Southern	Eastern
Number of bedrooms available	120	250	135
Room rates per night	$95	$124	$80
% bedroom occupancy	80%	75%	60%
Regional Bedroom Market share %	15%	16%	5%
Restaurant capacity per day (meals)	100	120	85
Restaurant utilisation	60%	40%	60%
Restaurant revenue	$876,000	$776,000	$837,000
Restaurant costs	$525,000	$945,000	$544,000
Hotel profit before tax	$832,000	$1,100,000	$576,000
Net Assets at 31 December	$4,200,000	$7,400,000	$4,400,000
Return on Net Assets	20%	15%	13%
Residual Income	$412,000	$360,000	$136,000

Task

Phil has sent you an email asking for information.

From:	Phil Webster PW@Lawco.co.uk
To:	Lee Ridley LR@Lawco.co.uk
Sent:	8th January 20X2, 10.24 a.m.

Subject: Hotel performance

Lee,

Thank you for the detailed information about each of the hotels but I now need a summary of the relative performance of the three hotels. How could performance be improved?

Kind regards,

Phil

Phil Webster

Managing Director

HTL

Write your response to the email from Phil Webster

One week later Phil sends you another email.

From: Phil Webster PW@Lawco.co.uk
To: Lee Ridley LR@Lawco.co.uk
Sent: 15ʰ January 20X1, 10.24 a.m.
Subject: Northern Hotel investment

Lee,

Investment Proposal

I am concerned about an investment proposal at the Northern Hotel. The manager is considering investing $800,000 in the construction of a leisure facility at the hotel. The hotel has permission to build the leisure facility, but will have to accept the terms of an agreement with the local community before beginning its construction.

The investment has a positive net present value of $225,000 when discounted at the group's cost of capital and is expected to generate additional annual profit for the hotel over the next five years. (See Exhibit 2)

- What do you think the effect of this investment will be on the future performance of the Northern Hotel? Do you think the hotel manager is likely to proceed with the investment?

Non-financial performance measures

On a separate note, I remember you telling me that non-financial performance measures are important in the service sector.

- Why is this and which two non-financial performance measures could HTL use to evaluate the performance of the hotel managers?

Kind regards,

Phil

Phil Webster

Managing Director

HTL

Exhibit 2

	Incremental net assets	Incremental Profit	Return on Net Assets
	$'000	$'000	%
20X2	750	110	14.7
20X3	700	120	17.1
20X4	650	155	23.8
20X5	600	145	24.2
20X6	550	130	23.6

Write your response to the email from Phil Webster

Task 5 - Alpha

(indicative timing excluding background information : 45 mins)

Background information

You are Kate Jones, a management accountant employed by the Alpha group which comprises two companies, X Limited and Y Limited both of which are resident in the same country.

X Limited has two trading divisions, a consultancy division which provides consultancy services to the engineering sector and a production division which assembles machinery which it sells to a number of industry sectors. Many of the components used in these machines are purchased from Y Limited. Y Limited manufactures components from raw materials many of which are imported. The components are sold globally.

Exhibit 1

Financial results at year end

	X Limited		Y Limited
	Consultancy division	Production division	
	$'000	$'000	$'000
External sales	710	1,260	400
Sales to X Limited			350
			750
Cost of sales	240	900*	250
Administration costs	260	220	130
Operating profit	210	140	370
Capital employed	800	2,000	4,000
ROCE	26.25%	7%	9.25%
Operating profit margin	29.6%	11.1%	49.3%
Asset turnover	0.89	0.63	0.19

*includes the cost of components purchased from Y Limited.

Task

Today is 20th May 20X5.

You have just received the following email from the Finance Director, Harry West

From:	Harry West HW@Alpha.co.uk
To:	Kate Jones KJ@Alpha.co.uk
Sent:	24th May 20X5, 10.08 a.m.

Subject: Transfer price problems

Kate,

A dispute has recently arisen between the managers of X Limited and Y Limited and I need you to do some analysis of what is going on.

As you probably know, the current policy of the group is to allow the managers of each company or division to negotiate with each other concerning the transfer prices.

The manager of Y Limited charges the same price internally for its components that it charges to its external customers. The manager of Y argues that this is fair because if the internal sales were not made he could increase his external sales. An analysis of the market demand shows that currently Y Limited satisfies only 80% of the external demand for its components.

The manager of the Production division of X Limited believes that the price being charged by Y Limited for the components is too high and is restricting X Limited's ability to win orders. Recently X Limited failed to win a potentially profitable order which it priced using its normal gross profit mark-up. The competitor who won the order set a price that was less than 10% lower than X Limited's price.

An analysis of the cost structure of Y Limited indicates that 40% of the cost of sales is fixed costs and the remaining costs vary with the value of sales.

Firstly, please could you:

- Provide me with a summary of the performance of each division of X Limited and of Y Limited and explain how the present transfer pricing policy is affecting the overall performance of the group.

Secondly, could you:

- Discuss the factors that should be considered when setting the transfer pricing policy and suggest a transfer pricing policy for the supply of the components from Y Limited to X Limited?

Kind regards,

Harry

Harry West

Finance Director

Alpha

E: HW@Alpha.co.uk

T: 0117 900100

Write your response to the email from Mr West.

Task 6 - NBL

(indicative timing excluding background information : 45 mins)

Background information

NBL manufactures parts for motor cars and its customers are car manufacturers who have been experiencing financial difficulties over the past few years. Sales have reduced significantly as a result of the worldwide economic recession. Costs have increased due to quality issues with parts that led to a recall of some models of cars.

NBL's management team is considering the purchase of machinery that would produce a new type of catalytic converter. However the level of demand for the new product is uncertain. As a result it commissioned a market research report which showed a pessimistic and an optimistic level of demand for the product.

Task

Today is 28th May 20X5. You are Paul Berry, a management accountant at NBL and have produced an investment appraisal for the new catalytic converter.

Exhibit 1

Pessimistic

	20X6 $	20X7 $	20X8 $	20X9 $
Machine	(480,000)			
Tax saved	18,144	14,878	12,200	55,578
Contribution		320,100	320,100	320,100
Fixed costs		(140,000)	(140,000)	(140,000)
Tax on extra profit		(37,821)	(37,821)	(37,821)
Working capital	(50,000)			50,000
Total cash flows	(511,856)	157,157	154,479	247,857
Discount factor 10%	1.000	0.909	0.826	0.751
PV	(511,856)	142,856	127,600	186,141
NPV	(55,259)			

Optimistic

	20X6 $	20X7 $	20X8 $	20X9 £
Machine	(480,000)			
Tax saved	18,144	14,878	12,200	55,578
Contribution		399,300	399,300	399,300
Fixed costs		(140,000)	(140,000)	(140,000)
Tax on extra profit		(54,453)	(54,453)	(54,453)
Working capital	(50,000)			50,000
Total cash flows	(511,856)	219,725	217,047	310,425
Discount factor 10%	1.000	0.909	0.826	0.751
PV	(511,856)	199,730	179,281	233,129
NPV	100,284			

$$\text{Average NPV} \quad \frac{(55,259)+100,284}{2} = \$22,513$$

Upon receipt of the appraisal you have prepared, Annie Holmes, a senior manager at NBL sends you the following e-mail:

To: Paul Berry BP@NBL.co.uk

From: Annie Holmes AH@NBL.co.uk

Sent: 28th May 20X5, 10.18 a.m.

Subject: Catalytic converter investment

Paul,

Thank you for the investment appraisal information you sent me. I have to admit that I know very little about the basis of your calculations and am unclear whether we should go ahead with this investment.

It would be very useful for me if you could send me an e-mail which:

- Explains in some detail what the figures in the tables mean (why can't we just look at the payback of the product?!)

- Are there any other ways in which we can analyse the risk and uncertainty of this investment, and what other factors should we consider before deciding to go ahead?

Many thanks,

Annie

Annie Holmes

Senior Manager

NBL

E: AH@NBL.co.uk

T: 0117 900100

Write your response to the email from Annie Holmes

Topic 4 – P2 Primary Tasks Solutions

Task 1

Marking scheme

	Marks	Marks
Explanation of target costing	Max 4	
2 marks per well explained point, and could include:		
Unable to dictate selling price/external focus		
Target cost and cost gap		
Explanation of kaizen costing	Max 4	
2 marks per well explained point, and could include:		
Continuous improvement		
How it could be implemented by ZZ		
Differences	2	
		_9_
Explanation of use of standard costing with kaizen		
2 marks per well explained point, and could include:	Max 8	
Reason why comparison is not meaningful		
Changing cost goals		
Controllability by managers		
Variance analysis		
		_8_
Costs of quality		
Prevention	2	
Appraisal	2	
Internal failure	2	
External failure	2	
		_8_
MAXIMUM FOR TASK		**25**

Suggested solution

Report to Mr Watts

Re: Falling margins

Purpose of Report:

This report will cover the following:

- How ZZ could use target costing and kaizen costing to improve its future performance, including an explanation of the differences between target costing and kaizen costing

- How ZZ can use standard costing and variance analysis to prepare meaningful reports when using kaizen costing

- How ZZ could analyse its costs of quality and reduce them

Target costing and Kaizen costing

Target costing is a costing system that can be used when a company is unable to dictate a selling price and is forced to accept the prevailing market selling price for a product. We know that we are operating in very competitive markets so this is particularly appropriate for ZZ.

We could apply target costing as follows. If the expected cost of the product already meets the target cost over its lifecycle, including any expected cost reductions, then production can commence. If the expected cost exceeds the target cost then a "cost gap" exists, and major changes should be introduced to reduce costs so that the target cost is achieved. If we cannot achieve the target cost then the product will be abandoned.

Kaizen costing has been used by some Japanese firms for over twenty years and is now widely used in the electronics and automobile industries. 'Kaizen' translates as continuous improvement, encouraging constant reductions in costs by tightening the 'standards'.

We could apply Kaizen costing as follows. The previous year's actual production cost serves as the cost base for the current year's production cost. A reduction rate and reduction amount are set. Actual performance is compared to the Kaizen goals throughout the year and variances are monitored. At the end of the current year, the current actual cost becomes the cost base for the next year. New (lower) Kaizen goals are set and the whole process starts again.

Differences

One of the main differences between the two methods is that target costing is applied before production commences, but Kaizen costing is applied after production has started.

Another difference is that target costing requires significant changes to be made, but Kaizen costing involves making a number of small improvements to the whole process as part of continuous improvement.

Standard costing and variance analysis

If we introduce Kaizen costing and make production changes based on that methodology, the true cost goals are continuously changing. Since standard cost is a static target, comparing the two for variance analysis purposes does not provide meaningful information.

In order to get more meaningful information, we could use the standard cost as the cost base for the current year's production cost. A reduction rate and reduction amount could then be set – these would be the Kaizen goals. In order for the variances being analysed to relate to the improvements from the introduction of Kaizen costing, the manufacturing costs being monitored should be the costs that are controllable by the managers. The other costs can be reported on separately.

Actual performance can be compared to the Kaizen goals throughout the year and variances monitored. At the end of the current year, the current actual cost will become the standard cost for the next year. New Kaizen goals will then be set and the whole process starts again.

Managers, having been involved in setting the Kaizen goals for cost reduction, and having introduced the improvements to the systems and processes, will be in a good position to evaluate the impact of the introduction of Kaizen costing, and whether any variances were due to operational issues or over/under-ambitious Kaizen goals.

Quality costs

Quality costs can be divided into costs of conformance and costs of non-conformance. Costs of conformance are the costs of achieving the specified quality standards.

Prevention costs could be incurred in operations – ensuring regular maintenance is carried out on manufacturing machinery to ensure output is of a consistent and high quality. This should reduce the costs associated with customers returning products under guarantee.

Appraisal costs could be incurred in outbound logistics – for example sample testing to ensure correct items reach customers on time and undamaged. Ensuring products are undamaged should reduce costs associated with customers returning products

Costs of non conformance are the costs of failure to deliver the required standard of quality.

Internal failure costs could occur in operations – for example if upon inspection some manufactured products were found to be faulty and therefore needed to be disposed of or reworked.

External failure costs could occur in service – if faulty production is undetected at the manufacturing stage, faulty grooming products may fail after delivery to customer (eg hair straightener heating elements may fail or catch fire) necessitating warranty claims handling procedures and incurring costs to correct these faults.

Higher spending on conformance costs should lead to lower costs of non-conformance.

Competency coverage

Sub-task	Technical		Business acumen	People		Leadership		Max
	Target costing, kaizen costing and the differences	9						9
	Standard costing v kaizen	8						8
	Costs of quality	8						8
Total		25						25

Task 2

Marking scheme

	Marks	Marks

Explanation of penetration v skimming
2 marks per well explained point, to include: Max 6
Penetration pricing
Skimming pricing
Application to Product R

Explanation of growth and maturity stages
2 marks per well explained point, to include: Max 7
Growth stage selling prices
Growth stage costs
Maturity stage selling prices
Maturity stage costs

Explanation of cost plus pricing
2 marks per well explained point, and could include: Max 6
Explanation of price
Disadvantages
Application to Product Q

Explanation of profit maximisation
2 marks per well explained point, and could include: Max 6
Explanation of model
Demand factors
Cost factors

MAXIMUM FOR TASK   **25**

Suggested solution

From: Sophie Best SB@PT.co.uk

To: Rachel Fisher RF@PT.co.uk

Sent: 8th June 2015, 11.12 a.m.

Subject: Pricing Strategies

Rachel,

Difference between penetration and skimming pricing strategies.

Penetration pricing is a policy of low prices when the product is first launched in order to obtain sufficient penetration into the market.

Product R is an innovative product and a strategy of penetration pricing could have been effective in discouraging potential new entrants to the market.

However, the product is believed to be unique and as such demand is likely to be fairly inelastic. In this instance a policy of penetration pricing could have significantly reduced revenue without a corresponding increase in sales.

Market skimming pricing involves charging high prices when a product is first launched and spending heavily on advertising and sales promotions to obtain sales.

The aim of market skimming is to gain high unit profits early in the product's life, allowing the costs of developing the product to be recovered.

Product R is new and different. A policy of market skimming appears most appropriate as customers are prepared to pay high prices for innovative products that are expected to change the market.

How unit selling prices and unit production costs change in the growth and maturity stages of the product life cycle.

Growth stage

Selling prices are likely to be decreasing for a number of reasons. The product will no longer be unique as competitors will be introducing their own versions of the product.

In an attempt to make the market less attractive to other companies PT may wish to lower their selling price and reduce the level of profitability on each unit. The selling price may also need to be lowered to attract different market segments to the product which will then lead to an increase in sales volume.

Production costs are also likely to decrease. Increasing production volume will give the opportunity to buy in greater bulk and take advantage of discounts which will reduce unit material costs,

Learning and experience curve effects may mean that direct labour will be more efficient which may reduce the direct labour cost.

Maturity stage

Selling prices are likely to reduce from the growth stage as the product has become established in the market, and the selling price is likely to remain fairly constant throughout this stage as the company looks to consolidate its position.

Direct labour costs are unlikely to reduce any further as the effect of the learning curve has ended.

Direct material costs are likely to remain fairly constant at this stage. Lower quantities of material may be required in comparison to the growth stage. This could reduce negotiating power with suppliers, leading to an increase in prices.

Overhead costs are likely to be similar to those at the end of the growth stage as optimum batch sizes have been established.

Disadvantages of 'total cost plus' pricing

Total cost plus pricing (also known as full cost plus pricing) is a method of determining sales price by calculating the total cost of a product or service and adding a percentage mark-up to that total cost for profit.

In a competitive environment such as that experienced by PT, the sales price is likely to be determined by the market. If the total cost plus price is below market price, the company is not maximising its profits. If the total cost plus price is above the market rate, sales demand will suffer which could lead to a vicious circle of lower sales creating higher unit costs (as fixed costs are split over fewer units) leading to higher prices and more drops in sales volume. This is illustrated by Product Q which is losing market share rapidly.

There is a disincentive to be more operationally efficient, as the profits increase as the costs increase. In a market that supports these costs the company can make more profit by being inefficient than by being efficient. Given the short product lifecycles, PT needs to make the maximum amount of profit possible in the time available for each product.

Disadvantages of setting prices based on profit maximisation.

The profit maximisation model assumes that price is the only determinant of demand. In reality other factors such as advertising, changes in trends or fashion, competitor activity and economic factors can influence demand.

The model assumes a static relationship between price and demand, but in practice this changes on a regular basis and is likely to be difficult to determine.

The profit maximisation model also assumes that variable costs all vary in line with volume but this is unlikely to be realistic as some of these costs will be driven by factors other than volume. The assumption that variable cost is unchanged once it has been determined may also not hold in the long run.

Please let me know if you have any questions or need any further information.

Kind regards,

Sophie

Accountant

PT

Competency coverage

Sub-task	Technical		Business acumen		People		Leadership		Max
	Penetration v skimming price	6							6
	Life cycle changes	7							7
	Cost plus pricing	6							6
	Profit maximisation	6							6
Total		**25**							**25**

Task 3

Marking scheme

	Marks	Marks
Explanation of problems		
2 marks per problem identified and explained	Max 8	
Suggested problems could include:		
Investing in new equipment		
Borrowing funds		
Inventory levels		
Recruitment of new employees		
Explanation of behavioural issues		
2 marks per issue identified and explained	Max 8	
Suggested issues could include:		
Damages relationships		
Lack of motivation		
Issues with decision making		
Explanation of Beyond Budgeting		
Up to 2 marks per well explained point, related to CW	Max 9	
Could include:		
Appropriate in the MBE		
Flexible culture		
Lack of rigid targets		
Use of benchmarks		
MAXIMUM FOR TASK		<u>25</u>

Suggested solution

From: Helen Black HB@CW.co.uk

To: Pippa Parker PP@CW.co.uk

Sent: 5th June 20X5, 2.45 p.m.

Subject: Budgets

The problems that could arise, for planning and decision making purposes within CW, if the store managers overstated their budgeted costs and resource requirements

Investing in new equipment

Overstating resource requirements may cause CW to invest in new equipment that is not actually required. This could reduce the funds available to invest in other areas of the business and could lead to cash flow problems.

<u>Borrowing funds</u>

In order to continue to fund the capital investment identified above, CW may need to enter into a loan facility with the bank. Such funding is not required but if used will result in CW incurring financing costs such as interest payments.

<u>Inventory levels</u>

CW may order excess items due to inaccurate budgets. As a result, inventory holding costs are likely to increase as products are not sold at the expected rate. Store managers may attempt to prove their budget was accurate by misappropriating items of inventory in the store accounts.

<u>Recruitment of new employees</u>

CW may recruit additional employees in order to meet budgeted resource requirements. This will lead to a needlessly high headcount, and increased payroll and training costs. When CW realise headcount is too high, they are likely to make employees redundant which will reduce morale within the workforce.

The behavioural issues that could arise if excess costs and resources are removed from the store managers' budgets

<u>Excess costs and resources removed with permission of the store manager</u>

Store managers are unlikely to agree that excess can be removed from the budget. By doing this they are effectively admitting that their original budget was inaccurate and that the budget was constructed with their own interests in mind at the expense of CW.

Admitting that the budget is inaccurate is likely to give the impression that they do not understand the operations and processes that are key to successfully running the store. As a result their ability to be a manager may be questioned.

<u>Excess costs and resources removed without the permission of the store manager</u>

Removal of costs and resources from the budget without consultation with the store manager will damage the relationships between CW management and the store managers.

Store managers may disown the revised budget and are unlikely to be motivated towards achieving it.

There is a risk that store managers will make operational decisions that cause adverse variances when compared to the revised budget in an attempt to prove that their original budget was more realistic.

How the principles of "Beyond Budgeting" promote a cultural framework that could be suitable for CW

The modern business environment is characterised by short product life cycles, fast technological advancements, intense competition, and customers who switch their suppliers frequently. In essence, the modern business environment is much less predictable and therefore a more flexible approach is required. In this kind of environment, it is dangerous to stick to a rigid course laid out in an annual budget, as those targets will more than likely be irrelevant very soon into the budgeting period.

What is required is a flexible, adaptive culture that reflects the pace and scope of change, and responds to change as it happens.

'Beyond Budgeting' involves not setting review targets, but rather communicating to a store as to what constitutes good performance, and assessing actual performance on an on-going basis and

in hindsight, bearing in mind the environment as it changes. It will promote an appropriate culture in several ways:

There is a lack of rigid targets, performance assessments are made with reference to the changing environment.

Performance assessments are made relative to external benchmarks, such as competitive performance. For example, it would be helpful to look at the market share of competitors' stores. This helps the organisation and individuals within it to understand their performance in context.

The actions required to achieve good performance are not explicitly laid out in 'Beyond Budgeting'. Principles of what constitutes good performance are communicated, nothing more. This is helpful if courses of action need to adapt and change to reflect the changing environment.

A picture of performance is built participatively, as often the subject of assessment (the Store Manager) knows more about the environment in which they operate than the assessor.

Given the modern environment is a 'buyers market', measuring quality and customer satisfaction becomes more important as targets than traditional performance measures. Customers may make their decision on where to shop based on a complex mixture of factors.

'Beyond budgeting' can target such measures more easily than the traditional budgeting approach, as it doesn't focus explicitly on budgeted financial information.

Competency coverage

Sub-task	Technical		Business acumen		People		Leadership		Max
	Problems with overstatement	8							8
					Behavioural issues	8			8
	Beyond Budgeting	9							9
Total		17				8			25

Task 4

Marking scheme

	Marks	Marks
Explanation of financial performance		
Overview/summary	Max 2	
Restaurant performance	Max 3	
Suggestions for improvement	Max 2	
Hotel room performance	Max 3	
Suggestions for improvement	<u>Max 2</u>	
Max for email 1		<u>12</u>
Explanation of investment decision		
NPV decision	Max 2	
RONA explanation	Max 3	
RONA decision	Max 1	
Explanation of non-financial performance measures		
Why they are important	Max 3	
2 marks per non financial measure suggested and explained	Max 4	
Max for email 2		<u>13</u>
MAXIMUM FOR TASK		<u>25</u>

Suggested solution

> From: Lee Ridley LR@HTL.co.uk
>
> To: Phil Webster PW@HTL.co.uk
>
> Sent: 9th January 20X2, 11.12 a.m.
>
> Subject: Hotel performance
>
> Phil,
>
> The Northern hotel has the highest return on net assets, and the Eastern hotel has the lowest. Eastern hotel's low RONA is caused by its poor occupancy rates, linked to its low market share. The performance of the Southern hotel would be enhanced by improvements to the profitability of its restaurant.
>
> Restaurants
>
> The Southern hotel is making a loss on its restaurant operation, the other two hotels are making a profit.
>
> The Southern restaurant serves fewer meals than the others, despite having a higher number of guests (a much greater room availability on a similar percentage occupancy to the other hotels).
>
> Depending on the cost profile of the restaurant the loss may be due to poor utilisation (if the costs are primarily fixed costs) or due to poor cost control (if the costs are largely variable costs).

The restaurant at the Southern hotel should consider its offer, for example, is it providing the right food at the price that customers are willing to pay? What competition is there – are there other restaurants near Southern but not the other hotels? Guest profile – do the hotel guests want to eat at the hotel or should Southern reduce its restaurant capacity?

Rooms

The hotels have different numbers of bedrooms, so it is not appropriate to compare them on the basis of their residual income values.

The differing prices being charged by the Northern and Southern hotels may be the effects of the market in each of those areas as the price difference does not seem to have significantly affected the market share achieved by each of the hotels and their high occupancy rates.

The Eastern hotel has a low market share (5%) and this might indicate that its room rate is badly priced or marketed. The low market share and occupancy rate might be due to other hotels offering cheaper accommodation, perhaps as loss leaders, or by the market being driven by a few key customers, such as large local companies, who have established relationships with other hotels in the region.

The Eastern hotel should consider a new marketing policy and examine its pricing compared to its competitors.

I hope that this helps, please contact me if you require further clarification.

Kind regards,

Lee

To: Phil Webster PW@HTL.co.uk
From: Lee Ridley LR@HTL.co.uk
Sent: 15ʰ January 20X2, 10.24 a.m.
Subject: Northern Hotel investment

Phil,

The investment has a positive net present value and yields a return in excess of the cost of capital of 10% in all years. It will therefore increase the value of the Northern hotel and of HTL. From a corporate perspective the investment should go ahead.

However, the manager of the Northern hotel gets a bonus payment based on the hotel's Return on Assets, so will probably make a decision based on how the investment will affect this payment. The RONA in the next year is lower than the 20% figure for 20X1, and will be for the following year as well. It is only in 20X4 that RONA rises above 20%, and while it improves the following year as well, it drops in 20X6. So although the investment is good for the company, it would mean that the manager might only receive a bonus in 2 of the 5 years of the facility.

The manager is unlikely to decide to proceed with the investment because it will reduce the bonus receivable.

Non-financial performance measures

Non-financial performance measures are important to companies such as HTL who operate in the service sector.

HTL will want to know how efficiently it operates and to measure the satisfaction levels of its guests which can directly affect its performance. For example if guests are unsatisfied this could cause bad word of mouth and reduce revenue for the year. By measuring satisfaction levels throughout the year, this gives opportunities to rectify the situation rather than waiting until revenue starts falling to realise that there is a problem. For this reason financial indicators are known as 'lagging measures' but non-financial indicators can be 'leading measures'.

It is also important not to focus on short-term measures to increase current financial performance that may decrease non-financial measures which may lead to lower profit levels in the longer term.

Customer complaints

A non-financial performance measure could be the number of customer complaints / suggested improvements. This may highlight poor service or short-cuts from managers that may potentially harm long-run profitability.

Use of hotel facilities

Another potential measure could be the rate of use of hotel facilities by residents and non-residents. This may indicate whether guests are making use of the hotel facilities and whether managers are making the range of facilities known to the guests and also whether they are successfully marketing the facilities outside of the hotels.

Kind regards,
Lee

Competency coverage

Sub-task	Technical		Business acumen		People		Leadership		Max
	Financial performance	12							12
	Investment decision and non-financial performance	13							13
Total		25							25

Task 5

Marking scheme

		Marks
Performance summary		
Discussion of consultancy division	2	
Comparison of Y and X Production Division	<u>4</u>	
		6
Explanation of transfer pricing policy		
2 marks per well explained point	Max	6
Could include:		
Behavioural implications		
Missed order for X		
Favouring of Y		<u>12</u>
Explanation of factors to consider		
2 marks per well explained point	Max	8
Could include:		
Reflection of capacity constraints		
External market demand		
Promote goal congruence		
Profit maximisation		
Suggested transfer pricing policy		
Market price	2	
Discount	1	
Variable cost	<u>2</u>	
		<u>13</u>
MAXIMUM FOR TASK		<u>**25**</u>

Suggested solution

From: Kate Jones KJ@Alpha.co.uk

To: Harry West HW@Alpha.co.uk

Sent: 25th May 20X5, 9.03 a.m.

Subject: Transfer price problems

Harry,

Summary of divisional performance and transfer pricing impacts

<u>Performance summary</u>

All divisions are profitable but the return on capital employed (ROCE) achieved by the Consultancy division of X (26.25%) is far higher than in other parts of the business.

As you know, the nature of consultancy businesses means that profits are often not derived from assets but from investing in high quality staff. As such, the level of capital investment required in consultancy businesses is relatively low.

The ROCE values of the Production division of X Limited (7%) and Y Limited (9.25%) are comparable. Y Limited has high unit profitability but the level of capital employed ($4m) is double that of the Production division. In contrast, the Production division is able to generate a high level of sales relative to its capital employed but has lower unit profitability.

Transfer pricing policy

Allowing the managers of each company or division to negotiate transfer prices with each other is likely to have a number of behavioural implications.

The current pricing policy does not benefit the Alpha group as a whole. X Limited recently missed out on a potentially profitable order due to high transfer prices charged by Y Limited. If Y Limited agreed to lower prices for components sold to X, it is likely that X Limited could pass this on to customers in the form of lower prices and thus win more orders.

The current policy also appears to favour Y Limited over X Limited so it is not surprising that this has created friction between the managers of each company.

The manager of Y Limited argues that the prices he charges X Limited are fair because if the internal sales were not made, he could increase external sales. This is not strictly true since Y Limited would have spare capacity if it did not sell to X.

Factors to consider and proposed transfer pricing policy

Factors to consider

The transfer price should provide an 'artificial' selling price that enables the transferring division to earn a return for its efforts, and the receiving division to incur a cost for benefits received.

Transfer prices should reflect capacity constraints and market demand for the item being transferred. The supplier's opportunity cost should be reflected in the transfer price.

The transfer price, if possible, should encourage profit centre managers to agree on the amount of goods and services to be transferred, which will also be at a level that is consistent with the aims of the organisation as a whole such as maximising company profits.

The Directors of Alpha Group could impose a transfer price, or oversee negotiations between the two companies. This however would reduce the autonomy of the two profit centre managers which could be demotivating and reduce the quality of decision making.

Suggested transfer pricing policy

Unsatisfied external demand for Y Limited is estimated at 20%. As such, it is reasonable that Y limited supplies some components to X Limited at the market price. X Limited may be able to negotiate a discount on the market price, given that selling internally effectively saves Y Limited administration and distribution costs incurred on external sales.

The remaining supplies to X Limited should be on a variable cost basis. X Limited may offer a slightly higher price as an incentive for Y to produce the components.

I hope that this helps, please ask if you need further information.

Kind regards,

Kate

Competency coverage

Sub-task	Technical		Business acumen		People		Leadership		Max
	Performance summary and transfer pricing policy impacts	12							12
							Factors to consider and suggested policy	13	13
Total		12						13	25

Task 6

Marking scheme

	Marks	Marks
Explanation of figures		
2 marks per well explained point, and could include:	Max 11	
Expected relevant cash flows		
Timing of cash flows		
Tax savings		
Discounted cash flows		
Increase in shareholder wealth		
Comment on payback	2	
		13
Explanation of risk and uncertainty		
2 marks per method explained, and could include:	Max 6	
Sensitivity analysis		
Simulation		
Increased discount rate		
Explanation of other factors		
2 marks per factor explained, and could include:	Max 6	
Technical feasibility		
Technical ability of existing employees		
Financing the project		
		12
MAXIMUM FOR TASK		25

Suggested solution

> To: Annie Holmes AH@PB.co.uk
>
> From: Paul Berry PB@PB.co.uk
>
> Sent: 25th May 20X5, 9.13 a.m.
>
> Subject: Catalytic converter investment
>
> **Explanation of figures**
>
> The calculations use the expected relevant cash flows associated with this investment based on an optimistic and pessimistic view of the contribution that it would generate. This contribution is the sales revenue less variable costs and the extra tax to be paid has also been calculated. Fixed costs will not change if production increases or decreases and it has been assumed that costs will not be affected by inflation.
>
> The machine will be paid for at the start of the investment and will generate tax savings as a result of tax allowable depreciation. It has been assumed that an additional $50,000 will be needed at the start for additional working capital finance, for example to build up inventory.
>
> The total cash flows for each year have then been discounted to present value using the company's cost of capital of 10%. This allows for the time value of money which is critical when

cash flows are going to be spread across several years. A project's cash flows need to be analysed to see if they offer a better return than an investor could get by investing elsewhere.

The discounted cash flows are added up and if the net present value (NPV) result is positive, this means that the project will increase shareholder wealth and is therefore acceptable. Using the optimistic estimates, the net present value is positive but using pessimistic estimates, it is negative.

The final figure of $22,513 is an average of the two NPV outcomes and assumes that each outcome is equally likely. It is an expected value which is not necessarily the most likely result and may not be a possible result.

It relates to cash flow not profit as accounting adjustments such as depreciation would be made calculate a net profit figure.

Payback

Payback is the time taken for cash inflows from a project to equal the cash outflows and the decision rule is to accept a project if its payback period is quicker than the company's target payback.

Payback can be used to assess risk as projects with a shorter payback period are considered to be less risky, but no account is taken of the time value of money and cash flows received or paid after payback are ignored. It is therefore simplistic and encourages short termism.

Risk and uncertainty, and other factors to consider

Risk and uncertainty

Other ways in which the risk and uncertainty of this investment could be analysed include using sensitivity analysis where one variable at a time is assessed to determine the percentage change necessary to reach a NPV of zero. The decision maker would then have more information on which to make a judgement.

In complex situations, simulation can be more useful as it uses a computer model to generate a range of possible outcomes. The decision to be made will then depend on attitude to risk.

If this project is viewed as particularly risky, the NPV analysis could be repeated using a higher discount rate in order to submit the project to a higher 'hurdle' test.

Other factors

NBL's customers have been struggling with falling sales and quality problems so it is essential to ensure that this investment will be worthwhile before committing resources to it.

The technical feasibility of the new type of catalytic converter must be thoroughly examined to ensure that there will not be any issues with the quality of the product. Any problems could affect NBL's image and reputation and hence its long term growth and survival prospects.

Do we have employees with sufficient technical ability to make the new product? Are the necessary supplies of raw materials available at the right price and quality? Is the new machine fully tested and ready to go or could there be delays whilst it is made ready for production?

Finally, we will need to decide how this project should be financed should the decision to go ahead be taken. It is obviously only feasible if we are able to raise sufficient funds at a suitable cost.

I hope that this helps, please ask if you need further information.

Kind regards,

Paul

Competency coverage

Sub-task	Technical		Business acumen		People		Leadership		Max
	Explanation of figures and commenting on payback	13							13
	Explanation of risk and uncertainty and other factors	12							12
Total		25							25

Topic 4 – P2 Further Tasks

Task 7 - TQ

Indicative timing – 54 mins (excluding background information)

Background information

You are Brenda Cole, a management accountant at TQ. TQ manufactures and retails electronic devices. The finance director Sarah Nolan sends you an email regarding TQ's newest product which is currently in development.

Task

From:	SN@tq.com
To:	BC@tq.com
Subject:	New product pricing and performance appraisal

Hello Brenda,

As you know, we are currently developing a new smart phone. It is a 'state of the art' phone with double the battery life of any other smart phone on the market, while maintaining the same functionality and sleek design.

We are really excited about this product, but we know that the technology for these products is advancing rapidly and that the life cycle for the product is relatively short. We've incurred a significant level of development costs.

The Board of Directors has now turned its attention to the pricing strategy that TQ should adopt for such a product.

Can you please respond to this email and:

- discuss the alternative pricing strategies available to TQ

A separate issue that will be discussed at the meeting is performance measurement. We have a set of very basic financial performance measures in place to periodically assess company performance. I am working on a report at the moment and I could really use your help.

Can you please respond to this email and:

- explain the value and use of non-financial performance measures
- discuss the relative merits of ROI and RI as performance measures

Thank you.

Regards,

Sarah Nolan

Please respond to Sarah.

Task 8 - MN Co

Indicative timing : 45 mins (excluding background information)

Background information

You are James Smith, a newly appointed management accountant at MN Co. MN Co manufactures automated industrial trolleys, known as TRLs.

In order to understand the manufacturing process, MN Co's Managing Director Katie Brown asks you to speak with the production manager Harry Carver. You take notes from that meeting.

Notes from meeting with Harry Carver, Production Manager (HC) 1/3/X5

Three different machines are used in the manufacture of TRL

- Machine X is old and unreliable and it breaks down from time to time.
- Machine Y is new and reliable
- Machine Z, which is old but reasonably reliable.

The bottleneck resource is time on machine Z. The throughput accounting ratio has been calculated at 1.84.

A just-in-time (JIT) system is in operation and it is company policy to hold minimal inventory of work-in-progress and no finished goods inventory from week to week.

The manufacturing process has not changed since the company was formed over 25 years ago.

There is a low staff turnover within the production department; some staff have been working there since the company was formed.

HC is confident that the production department is as efficient as possible, and that this is due to the experienced staff.

HC knows that that you could source cheaper component parts from other suppliers but believes that this is a bad route to go down, even if it might appear to make financial sense on the face of it.

HC notes that previous "overly enthusiastic" management accountants have tried to bring in new cost control measures, but it's usually just a "passing fad that never really goes anywhere." All he wants from the finance department is to sign off on the replacement of new machinery when it's required, and leave the production process to him.

Kate Brown takes a look at your notes, and sends you the following email

Task

Dear James,

I see that you had an interesting meeting with Harry.

Harry is very experienced, but a little bit resistant to input from other parts of the business.

I would like the finance department to work closer with the production department and I think that you can help me with this task. You should note that Harry is not completely resistant to change, and I can see that he is now using a system of throughput accounting to monitor the production process. This was put in place by the previous management accountant, but I must admit that I am no expert. You might be able to help me by responding with the following information.

- Briefly describe the uses to which advocates of throughput accounting suggest that the ratio be put and suggest two other ratios which may be used by a company operating throughput accounting and explain the use to which they may be put.

- Explain how the concept of contribution in throughput accounting differs from that in marginal costing.

I note that Harry is aware of the availability of cheaper components which could be used in the manufacture of TRLs. I'm interested to know why Harry might think it is a "bad route" to go down, even if it makes financial sense.

- Perhaps you could explain two non-financial factors that should be considered before deciding whether or not to manufacture the component internally.

Thanks,

Kind regards,

Kate Brown MD

Please respond to Kate

Task 9 - LCG

Indicative timing (excl. background information) : 1ˢᵗ email – 30mins, 2ⁿᵈ email – 15mins

Background information

You are Elizabeth Cresswell, and you have recently been appointed management accountant of LCG. LCG designs and assembles electronic devices to allow transmission of audio / visual communications between the original source and various other locations within the same building.

Task

You receive the following email from the Managing Director Paul Lambert.

> Dear Elizabeth,
>
> Welcome to LCG! Like you, I am new to the job and I'm keen to hit the ground running.
>
> I am increasingly concerned about the trends in falling sales volumes, rising costs and hence declining profits over the last two years. There is general agreement amongst the managers of LCG that these trends are the result of the increasingly intense competition that has emerged over the last two years. LCG continues to have a reputation for high quality but this quality is now being matched by the competition.
>
> The competitors are eroding LCG's share of the market by selling equivalent products at lower prices. It is thought that in order to offer such low prices the production costs of the competitors must be lower than LCG's.
>
> I know that you have recently completed your CIMA studies and are familiar with the use of functional analysis.
>
> - Can you advise me how LCG could improve its sales volumes, costs and profits by using functional cost analysis?
>
> On another matter, I recently attended a presentation on world class manufacturing entitled 'The extension of the value chain to include suppliers and customers'.
>
> It all sounded great, but I am not sure it could be applied to LCG. Can you explain for me the following:
>
> - The components of the extended value chain and how each of the components may be applied by LCG.
>
> Kind regards,
>
> Paul

Please respond to Paul's email

A short while later you receive the following email from Karen Hart, the production manager:

Dear Elizabeth,

I know that you are just starting here at LCG but the new managing director Paul is leaving no stone unturned in his quest to cut costs and increase profits! He is looking at every aspect of the business, and yesterday he turned his attention to our inventory holding costs.

LCG currently uses a constant flow production system to manufacture our components. Demand from customers is higher in certain months of the year and lower in others. LCG holds inventory so that it can supply the components as they are demanded. Increasingly, the costs to LCG of holding inventory are having a significant effect on its profits and Paul is considering changing the production system to one that operates on a just-in-time (JIT) basis.

I'm a little bit concerned as I don't know much about JIT, but I have heard that it might not necessarily increase profits, and since that is Paul's aim, I am afraid that I might be blamed for that!

Can you help me out by:

- Explaining the concepts of a JIT production system and explaining two reasons why the profit of LCG may not increase as a result of changing to a JIT production system.

Thank you in advance for your help.

Kind regards,

Karen

Please respond to Karen

Task 10 - CNJ

Indicative timing – 45 mins (excluding background information)

Background information

You are Jane Sears, the management accountant at CNJ. CNJ operates a chain of fitness clubs. The clubs are structured into two divisions, the Eastern division and the Western division. Each division has a Managing Director who is responsible for revenue, cost and investment decisions at their clubs.

Task

You receive the following email from Martin Roche, the managing director.

Dear Jane,

We are currently assessing the key performance measures of management at CNJ.

- Can you please review the attachment (exhibit 1) which contains some key performance measures, and comment on the performance over the two year period using any four measures.

Note that a bonus is awarded each year to the Managing Director that generates the higher return on capital employed (ROCE).

There is another issue that concerns me. Investigations by CNJ's audit team have revealed that at the end of 20X1 the Managing Director of the Western Division rejected the opportunity to acquire a new building and equipment to set up a new fitness club at a total cost of $800,000. The investment would have taken place on 1 January 20X2. The project's estimated return on investment was 20.3%. Taking on the investment would have resulted in a ROCE of 32% for the division. However, the NPV calculated for the project was $158,000. I am perplexed by this decision, but our finance director has said that this shows the key limitation of using ROCE as a divisional performance measure.

- Can you please explain what she meant by this?

For many years the division managers have been asked by the Operations Director to prepare a budget for their divisions as part of the company's annual budgeting process. A divisional manager has been appointed to the Eastern division and he has concerns about the validity of these annual budgets. He argues that they soon become out of date as operational circumstances change. At a recent manager's meeting he said, 'They are restrictive. They do not permit the divisional managers to make decisions in response to operational changes, or change working practices for next year until that year's budget has been approved.'

- Can you explain the differences between the above annual budgeting system and a rolling budget system and discuss how the Eastern divisional manager could use a rolling budget system to address his concerns

Kind regards,

Martin

Please respond to Martin's email

Exhibit 1

The following summary information shows the results of the divisions for the past two years:

	20X2 Eastern	20X2 Western	20X1 Eastern	20X1 Western
ROCE %	38.0	41.7	29.3	26.7
Operating profit margin %	10.6	15.1	11.6	14.2
Asset turnover (time)	3.6	2.8	2.5	1.9
Staff costs/revenue %	63.9	57.7	62.1	58.2
Op costs-depreciation/revenue %	11.7	15.1	13.2	14.2
Staff costs $	1,150,000	1,430,000	1,180,000	1,310,000
Revenue per member $	265	267	266	267
Staff costs per member $	169	154	165	156

Task 11 - Pathology Laboratory

Indicative timing (excl. background information) : 1ˢᵗ email – 30mins, 2ⁿᵈ email – 15mins

Background information

You are Charlie Long, a newly appointed management accountant at The Pathology Laboratory service of the County Hospital which provides diagnostic services to support the care provided by the County Hospital, local General Practitioners, other hospitals and healthcare providers.

On your first day, you are given some literature to read about the company. You are drawn to comments made by the Head of the laboratory, Bill Smith, about the importance of the work done by the Pathology Laboratory:

> "Over 70% of diagnostic and treatment decisions made by doctors are based on medical laboratory test results. Without our work, doctors would not be able to confirm their diagnosis. Laboratory results give us the ability to identify diseases in their earliest stages so that we have a better chance of treating people effectively. The types of tests performed by our highly-trained staff encompass the entire spectrum of human disease, from routine diagnostic services to clinical laboratories that specializes in bone marrow transplants. The laboratories provide over four million tests each year, providing doctors with the information needed for diagnosis and treatment of all kinds of condition. Our vision is to continually improve the efficiency of the laboratory to ensure the best economic approach to patient care."

Shortly after reading this, you receive an email from Sally Dunn, MD.

Task

Dear Charlie,

The management team of the County Hospital has decided that the use of the balanced scorecard should be cascaded down to departmental level. Consequently, departmental managers have been given the task of designing a balanced scorecard for their departments.

- Can you please recommend an objective and a suitable performance measure for each of the three non-financial perspectives of a balanced scorecard that the Pathology Laboratory could use.

Note. In your response, please state three perspectives and then recommend an objective and a performance measure for each one of your three perspectives.

I wonder if you also could help me with a couple of budgeting control queries that I have.

The budget control system used last year operated as follows: I estimated the demand for the year for each department. Each department manager then prepared a cost budget based on the demand estimate for the division. These budgets were then submitted to me for approval. I then amended them before issuing each departmental manager with the final budget for the department. I didn't discuss these amendments with the respective departmental managers.

Actual performance was then measured against the final budgets for each month and each departmental manager's performance was appraised by asking the departmental manager to explain the reasons for any variances that occur.

The Corporate manager was asked to explain why her staff costs exceeded the budgeted costs for last month while the chargeable time was less than budgeted. She is not happy with the budgeting system stating that 'it focuses on financial performance and ignores the other performance indicators found in modern performance management systems'.

It appears that she is not the only one who is dissatisfied with the current system. As you are new to your position, I feel I could benefit from some fresh observation.

- Can you please provide me with some feedback on the present budgeting system and its likely effect on departmental manager motivation?

Kind regards

Sally Dunn

Please respond to Sally.

Later, you receive an email from Lauren Forde, the Director of Research and Development in County Hospital.

Dear Charlie,

Sally told me that you are doing a bit of work around the area of budgeting for her. This is an area that I, as Director of R&D feel really strongly about.

The Research and Development Division is finding it extremely difficult to maintain its current levels of achievement. The Division is suffering from a lack of funds as a result of the current budgeting system. We receive an uplift of 5% each year from the previous year's budget. This does not provide the necessary funds or freedom to be able to keep us on the cutting edge of healthcare technology and developments. In the past we were considered world leaders in the area of diagnostics. I would like to see incremental budgeting replaced by zero based budgeting in my division.

I am confident that it will be advantageous, however, the previous management accountant told me that I would regret pushing for ZBB. I am not sure why exactly.

- Can you please discuss the potential disadvantages of implementing zero based budgeting for the allocation of funds to the Research and Development Division from my perspective?

Kind regards,

Lauren

Please respond to Lauren

Task 12 - Beauty Co

Indicative timing – 45 mins (excluding background information)

Background information

You are Hilda Byrne, a newly appointed management accountant for Beauty Co. Beauty Co manufactures perfumes and cosmetics by mixing various ingredients in different processes, before the items are packaged and sold to wholesalers.

Jeff Thomas, the production manager has sent you the following report on the production process.

Process B

This is the first process. Raw materials are blended to produce three different outputs, two of which are transferred to Processes C and D respectively. The third output is accounted for as a by-product and sold in the external market without further processing. The equipment used to operate this process originally cost $800,000 on 1 January 20X5.

Process C

This process receives input from Process B to which is added further materials to produce a finished product that is sold in the external market. The equipment used to operate this process originally cost $500,000 on 1 January 20X8.

Process D

This process receives input from Process B which is further processed to produce a finished product that is sold in the external market. The equipment used to operate this process originally cost $300,000 on 1 January 20X0.

For all three processes, the material costs are variable per unit of input and direct labour costs are fixed in the short term because employees' contracts provide them with a six month notice period. Overhead costs include a share of Head Office costs, and of the remaining overhead costs some vary with the input volume of the process. Transfer prices between the processes are based on total budgeted cost plus 15%.

Today you have received the following email from Ruth Malone, the Managing Director.

Task

Dear Hilda,

Welcome to Beauty Co. It is great to have you on board. At Beauty Co we use a divisional structure with each process being regarded as a separate division with its own manager who is set performance targets at the start of each financial year which begins on 1 January. Performance is measured using return on investment (ROI) based on net book value of capital equipment at the start of the year.

The annualised ROI achieved by each of the process divisions during April 20X0 is calculated as follows:

Process	Profit / (Loss) ($)	Capital value	Month ROI	Annualised ROI
Process B	18,800	$800,000 \times 0.8^5 = \$262,144$	7%	84%
Process C	(15,550)	$500,000 \times 0.8^2 = \$320,000$	(5%)	(60%)
Process D	(5,000)	$300,000 \times 0.8^{10} = \$32,212$	(15%)	(180%)

Some of the divisional managers believe that this is an unsuitable performance measure for Beauty Co.

- Do you agree with them, in the context of the data provided for each process division? If so, why?

As well as performance measures, some managers are dissatisfied with the current transfer pricing policy. Output transferred from one process to another is valued using transfer prices based on the total budgeted costs of the process plus a mark-up of 15%.

The current transfer price from Process B is $9.20. The manager of Process D believes that the transfer price from Process B is unfair because the equivalent material could be purchased in the open market at a cost of $7·50 per litre.

- Can you help me assess this situation by discussing the transfer pricing policy being used by H from the viewpoints of the managers of Process Division B and Process Division D?

Perhaps you might also be able to advise me in the area of cost reduction. It has come to my attention that our traditional absorption costing system is focused on cost containment rather than cost reduction. I have heard that modern, activity based, cost management focuses on process improvement and the identification of how processes can be more effectively and efficiently performed to result in cost reductions.

- Can you advise me how activity based management differs from the traditional cost containment approach and how it seeks to achieve cost reduction?

Kind regards,

Ruth

Please respond to Ruth.

Topic 4 – P2 Further Tasks Solutions

Task 7

Marking scheme

		Marks
(1)	Discussion of pricing strategies (2 marks per valid point)	10
(2)	Value and use of NFPM (2 marks per valid point)	10
	ROI and RI explained and compared	10
		30

Suggested solution

> **To:** SN@tq.com
> **From:** BC@tq.com
> **Subject:** New product pricing and performance appraisal
>
> Here is the information you requested.
>
> **Market skimming**
>
> This strategy involves charging **high prices when a product is first launched** and spending heavily on advertising to obtain sales to exploit any price insensitivity in the market. As the product moves into **later life cycle stages, prices can be reduced.** The aim is therefore to gain high profits early in the product's life. This would be useful for us as it would generate **high initial cash flows** needed to cover the significant development costs we have incurred.
>
> A **high price** makes it more likely that **competitors** will **enter** the market, however, and so there must be significant **barriers to entry** or the product must be **differentiated** in some way. The fact that our product is 'state of the art' should provide some level of differentiation. High prices could therefore be charged to take advantage of its **novelty appeal**.
>
> **Market penetration pricing**
>
> This is a policy of **low prices when a product is first launched** in order to **achieve high sales** volumes and hence **gain a significant market share.** If we adopt this strategy it might **discourage competitors** from entering the market.
>
> Smartphones are considered to be a luxury product, and as such, our **product** is likely to be **elastic. Penetration pricing** is most suited to products for which demand is **elastic** and so responds well to low prices.
>
> **Demand-based approach**
>
> This approach is based on the **assumption that there is a profit-maximising combination of price and demand** because demand is elastic. We would need to commission some market research if we were to adopt such a strategy, however, to obtain information about levels of demand at various prices.

However, there are several **drawbacks** to this approach. For example, it can be difficult to predict the demand curve, even with market research. Also, it assumes that price is the only influence on the quantity demanded. Other factors such as quality of the product, levels of after sales service and so on could also impact.

Premium pricing

This involves making a product appear 'different' so as to justify a premium price. For us, this strategy would involve highlighting the product's 'state of the art' features as a **differentiating factor**.

Premium prices will always be paid by those customers who blindly equate high price with high quality.

Price discrimination

A **different price** for the product would be charged to **different groups of buyers** if this strategy were adopted. There are a number of bases on which such discriminating prices can be set.

In our case, we could charge a different price if the product were bought on-line to the price charged in retail outlets.

Value and use of non-financial performance measures

It is argued that management should not focus on a **narrow** range of performance measures, such as maximising **short-term** profits as this may damage the longer-term objectives of shareholder value maximisation.

A full range of performance measures are required to obtain a **complete picture** of long-term success. In order to achieve the long-term objectives of shareholder value maximisation and profit growth, the company must produce quality goods or services at a price customers are willing to pay. Factors such as **quality control, customer satisfaction, innovation, efficiency** and **staff development** are elements that determine long term success.

Advantages

The value of non-financial measures is that they **draw management attention to some of the more strategic issues facing the organisation**. Financial measures tend to make managers more inward looking and may encourage them to focus on short-term performance. Non-financial measures can be selected to encourage managers to **think strategically** and **consider external factors** such as competitor actions and customer requirements.

Examples

Examples of non-financial measures include market share and market leadership, innovation, efficiency, productivity, customer satisfaction, service and staff development.

Problems

One problem with implementing some of these measures is that they may be **difficult to record objectively**. For example, assessing staff development may involve measuring the number of days training per member of staff. However, the training may not have been effective in developing staff in any meaningful way. If performance measurement is perceived to be subjective, **this could lead to dysfunctional behaviour**. For example, management may only make decisions which will increase divisional ROI regardless of the wider corporate benefits.

> **ROI v RI**
>
> ROI
>
> The ROI is a relative performance measure calculated as (profit before interest/investment) × 100%.
>
> The ROI can sometimes lead to **sub-optimal decisions** if applied too rigidly. For example, an investment may be rejected if it lowers the centre's actual ROI, even though it earns more than the company's required return on capital.
>
> RI
>
> RI can **overcome this problem** since it rewards all investments which earn a return higher than the company's required return on capital.
>
> RI is the profit before interest minus imputed interest charge on centre investment.
>
> The **imputed interest** is calculated at the rate of the company's required return on capital. The residual income will always increase if an investment earns more than the company's required rate or return.
>
> RI can therefore overcome some of the behavioural problems associated with ROI. RI is also more flexible since a different cost of capital can be applied to investments with different risk characteristics.
>
> However, its weakness is that it does not facilitate comparisons between investment centres.
>
> **ROI** is intended to measure the efficiency with which assets are being used, by taking the profit as a proportion of the net assets. **RI** on the other hand, is simply the profit reduced by a financing charge which is based on the net assets. RI is an absolute, not a relative measure.
>
> **ROI,** therefore has the major advantage of taking full account of the size of the business, so that **businesses of different sizes can be compared. Income**, on the other hand, may be **less distorted by inappropriate values for investment.**
>
> Kind regards,
>
> Brenda Cole.

Competency coverage

Sub-task	Technical		Business acumen	People		Leadership		Max
1	Pricing strategies	10						10
2	Non-financial performance	10						10
3	Financial performance	10						10
Total		30						30

Task 8

Marking scheme

		Marks	
(1)	Throughput accounting		
	Uses of TA ratio (2-3 marks per valid point.)	4-5	
	Two other suitable ratios with explanation (2-3 marks each)	4-5	Max 9
(2)	TA vs. marginal costing (2 -3 marks per valid point.)		8
(3)	Non financial factors in make or buy decision (1-2 marks per factor)		8
			25

Suggested solution

Dear Kate,

Thank you for your email, please find the response to your queries outlined below.

The following **uses** for the throughput accounting ratio have been suggested.

- In a throughput environment, production priority must be given to the products best able to generate throughput, that is those products that maximise throughput per unit of key or bottleneck resource. The throughput accounting ratio can be used to **rank products**, the product with the highest value of this ratio being given the highest ranking.

- The throughput accounting ratio compares the rate at which a product earns contribution with the rate at which production costs are incurred. If the ratio is greater than one, contribution is being generated at a rate faster than that at which production costs are being incurred. The opposite is true if the ratio is less than one. The ratio can therefore be used to determine **whether or not a product should be produced**.

Two other ratios which may be used by a company operating throughput accounting

- **Schedule adherence**. This will highlight how well production schedules are being adhered to.
  - (i)   Given that products should not be made unless there is a customer waiting for them, it is vital that production is not disrupted otherwise the customer will be kept waiting.
  - (ii) Given that the ideal work in progress level is zero and buffer stocks are not held, it is vital that production schedules are kept to, otherwise the entire production process will come to a halt.

- **First-time capability (especially of output from the bottleneck process).** Below quality output at the bottleneck process would use up valuable resource time to transform it into saleable output, thereby reducing throughput capacity and increasing costs.

Contribution differences under marginal costing and throughput accounting

The underlying concepts between marginal costing (MC) and throughput accounting (TA) are the same in that both are based on the concept of contribution and consider variable costs only. In both approaches, the contribution earned can be used **to assess the relative earning capabilities of different products** in order to determine an optimum production mix.

However, the concept of contribution is not the same under the two concepts. This is because TA and MC define variable costs in different ways.

Throughput accounting takes a more extreme view than MC and considers only direct materials as variable costs. This is based on the idea that labour costs are not variable in the short term and are therefore ignored when calculating contribution. Throughput accounting is therefore often referred to as 'super variable costing'.

TA is based on the underlying concepts of the 'Theory of constraints' that seeks to maximise throughput by identifying binding constraints in a production system. To achieve evenness of production the 'Theory of constraints' aims to identify and remove bottlenecks where possible. Output through the binding constraint should never be delayed or held up or sales will be lost. To avoid this happening, a buffer inventory should be kept prior to the binding constraint.

Non-financial factors

There are a number of non-financial factors that should be considered when making a decision on whether to produce a component internally or to purchase from an external supplier.

Impact on employee morale

Outsourcing the manufacture of the component might have a favourable financial impact, however if in-house staff are underused (or even made redundant) it would be important to consider the impact on staff morale who might feel that their jobs are under threat.

Control

MN may prefer to control / oversee the production of the component and may not wish to be dependent on a third party for delivering the component on time and with adequate quality. MN has manufactured all the components of the TRLs for 25 years, therefore its customers must be confident that the product is made up of high quality components.

Impact on community

Using an external supplier may result in job losses. This may affect the local community, particularly if the new external supplier is not local.

Quality

It is very hard to assess whether the quality provided by an external supplier will be the same as the current quality. At present there is a low staff turnover and therefore staff are loyal and experienced. This may not be the case with the staff of the external supplier and therefore the quality of the component may drop.

I trust that the above information answers your queries, however, should you have any further queries please don't hesitate to contact me.

Kind regards,

James Smith

Competency coverage

Sub-task	Technical		Business acumen	People		Leadership		Max
1	Throughput accounting	9						9
2	TA vs. Marginal costing	8						8
3				Non financial factors in make/buy decision	8			8
Total		17				8		25

Task 9

Marking scheme

		Marks
(1)	Functional analysis explanation (up to 2 marks per point) Benefit of functional analysis to LCG (up to 2 marks per point)	10
(2)	The components of the extended value chain (up to 2 marks per point) Application to LCG (up to 2 marks per point)	10
(3)	Concepts of JIT system (up to 2 marks per point) Effect on profitability (up to 2 marks per point)	10
		30

Suggested solution

Dear Paul,

Please find below the response to your queries.

Functional cost analysis

Functional cost analysis is concerned with **improving profits by attempting to reduce costs** and / or by **improving products** by adding new features in a cost-effective way. Functional analysis is typically used prior to the **production of new products**.

A new product is analysed into its **component parts**, and the function of each separate component is specified in simple terms. Alternative ways of creating the same value with **cheaper components**, or **creating more value** without adding to cost, are then considered. Where **better design alternatives are found**, they should be adopted.

How functional cost analysis can benefit LCG

Reducing costs

Functional cost analysis could help LCG to **reduce costs of new products**. If new products can be produced at a lower cost and sold at a market price, the lower costs will lead to higher profits.

For example, ways may be identified to reduce the number of components in the product, reduce packaging, remove unnecessary components, use less expensive materials or different methods of transportation and so on. Lower product costs will create an opportunity to sell products at a lower price, and this should result in higher sales volumes.

Value and demand

If more value can be built into a new product within a target unit cost, **customer demand** for the product at a given price **should be stronger**, and LCG may be able to sell the product at a higher price, or a larger volume at a lower price.

The biggest value gains and financial benefits are often achieved at the **design stage** of a product's life cycle. LCG should start by assessing the value provided by each component part of the product. The **value created** by each component is then **compared** with the **value it will provide** to the customer.

Value chain

The aim of the **value chain** is to maximise **value** creation while minimising costs. The **value chain** is the sequence of business **activities** by which, from the **perspective of the end user, value is added** to the products and services produced by an entity. These activities are known as **primary** and **support** activities and are value activities.

The **primary activities** include: inbound logistics, operations (production), outbound logistics, sales and marketing, and service (maintenance). The **support activities** include: administrative infrastructure management, human resources management, R&D, and procurement.

<u>Costs and value drivers are identified for each **value** activity</u>

The idea of the value chain has been **extended** beyond individual organisations. Where this occurs, the value chain is known as an **extended value chain**, and it can apply to whole supply chains and distribution networks. Individual value chains combine to deliver value to the end user.

The elements of LCG's extended value chain would be **its suppliers, distributors and customers**.

Suppliers

LCG could examine its **relationships with suppliers of parts** in its electronic devices. For example, **using supply chain management**. This involves looking at ways of **improving the supply chain**. For instance LCG could switch to new suppliers by purchasing on-line.

LCG could require its part suppliers to be located nearby its assembly plant to minimise the transportation costs. The company could also consider tying its suppliers into a JIT agreement to keep inventory levels to a minimum, saving on stockholding costs. However this does need to be balanced against the risks of stock-outs and damaging relationships with customers.

LCG could try to **negotiate cheaper prices** for the components it buys in. Furthermore, the organisation could agree quality standards and inventory levels with its suppliers, thereby **building in quality without increasing cost**.

Retailers and customers

LCG should look at price and could consider **negotiating better margins** on its products, or consider **undertaking some market research** prior to development of new products to establish exactly what the customer sees as a quality product. This would control research costs and direct effort to where value is added. It could also **reduce the complexity of products** being offered if some of these aren't selling. LCG should also consider the transport costs and reliability of supplying its product to customers.

Other ideas

- LCG could **share technology** with suppliers and streamline its expertise.

- LCG could consider **outsourcing** activities that aren't **core**.

- LCG could standardise components and products so it **reduces complexity** without compromising on product availability.

Should you have any further queries in respect of the above please don't hesitate to contact me.

Kind regards,

Elizabeth Cresswell

Dear Karen,

Please find below the response to your query regarding JIT systems.

Just-in-time production is a production system which is **driven by demand** for finished products whereby each component on a production line is **produced only when needed** for the next stage.

The objective is to produce or to **procure products** or components **as they are required** (by a customer or for use) rather than for inventory.

This will mean that ideally for LCG there will be:

No inventories at any stage including no finished goods inventory as items will be completed just as they are to be delivered to customers.

A system in place so that there is **no work in progress** between the different stages of production.

Changing to a JIT production system will not necessarily improve the profitability of LCG, at least in the short term for several reasons which include the following.

Purchase discounts

As there will be no holdings of inventory LCG will **not be purchasing components in bulk** and will lose out on potential **bulk purchase discounts** as it will need to have more frequent and smaller orders.

If the increased ordering and delivery costs are greater than the reduced inventory holding costs then PR will not be more profitable.

Overtime

As production needs to be **timed to match demand** (which fluctuates), at times of higher demand it may be necessary to work **overtime**.

Overtime is likely to be **paid at a premium rate** which may make **labour costs higher** than the constant flow production system.

Kind regards,

Elizabeth Cresswell

Competency coverage

Sub-task	Technical		Business acumen		People		Leadership		Max
1	Functional analysis	10							10
2			Value chain	10					10
3	JIT system and the effect on profitability	10							10
Total		20		10				6	20

Task 10

Marking scheme

Suggested solution

Dear Martin,

Thank you for your email, please find my response to your query outlined below.

Performance measures

ROCE

The Eastern division generated the highest ROCE in 20X1 and the manager of Eastern would be awarded the bonus for that year. In 20X2 however this is reversed and the Western divisional manager would be awarded the bonus. The percentage ROCE has increased markedly for each division, but operating profits as a percentage of revenue have not. This increase in ROCE is driven by the increasing age (and therefore lower net book value) of capital employed. This shows through as higher asset turnover, while operating profit as a percentage of revenue has remained fairly consistent.

Staff costs

In Eastern, these have increased over the period as a percentage of revenue and per head but have decreased in Western. This is to be expected given staff costs are probably relatively fixed, and volumes have increased in Western and fallen in Eastern.

Revenue per member

This has remained fairly consistent – meaning spending patterns amongst members has not changed. It is uncertain whether the mix of their spending (eg gym v refreshments) has varied over the period.

Other operating costs (less depreciation)

As a percentage of revenue, these have fallen in Eastern and increased in Western. This may indicate improving cost control in Eastern as a management response to falling revenues.

Limitations of ROCE

The manager of the Western division is assessed using the ROCE of his division. He will therefore accept a project that will increase the reported divisional return on capital employed. By taking on the project, the manager would reduce the divisional ROCE from 41.7% and so would reject the project. If he were to accept the project the Divisional ROCE would be lower at 32%.

Given the way performance is measured, the manager is in this case encouraged to make a goal incongruent decision. The project would benefit the division, and the group as a whole, however it would negatively affect the manager's bonus. Therefore, despite having a positive net present value, the project was rejected.

Further limitations of ROCE include:

The risk of goal incongruent decisions (per above.)

It is a relative measure so does not measure the impact on shareholder wealth of that division's performance.

It is affected significantly by depreciation policy and the age of assets rather than fundamental performance.

It ignores the time value of money.

Rolling budget system vs annual budget system

A rolling budget system is a system of budgeting that is continuously updated by adding a further accounting period (a month or quarter) when the earlier accounting period has expired.

An annual budgeting system is a system under which budgets are prepared for a 12 month period, usually running to the end of the financial year of the company.

A key difference between the two systems is that managers using a rolling budget system view it as a necessary planning and control procedure that takes place on a regular basis, not as a separate exercise that is used to monitor and measure their performance.

The manager of the Eastern division is concerned that the current annual budgeting system is restrictive and does not enable managers to make decisions in response to operational decisions or working practices. For example, budgets for the coming year may not be approved until close to the start of the next year. As a result, managers are likely to find that they do not have the authority to make decisions relating to next year until the year has almost commenced.

Under a rolling budget system, it is likely that each update to the budget will be approved by the Board of Directors. In this scenario, managers will have the authority to make decisions in line with the approved budget for the next 12 months or more.

If CNJ introduced a system of rolling budgets, it would enable divisional managers to plan ahead and make key decisions in a timely manner. For example, managers would know how much money is available to recruit new staff within the next 12 month period.

The new manager also argues that annual budgets quickly become out of date as circumstances change. If a rolling budget system employed by CNJ allows the budget for the remaining part of the current budget year to be revised, it will combat the new manager's argument.

If this is the case, care must be taken to ensure that the system does not allow managers to eliminate variances caused by actual performance. Any variances from the approved budget should be fully investigated

Should you have any further queries please don't hesitate to contact me.

Kind regards,

Jane

Competency coverage

Sub-task	Technical		Business acumen		People		Leadership		Max
	Financial performance measures and limitations of ROCE	16							16
	Annual and rolling budget systems	9							9
Total		25							25

Task 11

Marking scheme

			Marks
(1)	Three non financial measures		
	Objective (1 mark per measure)	3	
	Application (1 mark per measure)	3	
	Measure (1 mark per measure)	3	
			9
(2)	Participative budgeting		
	2 marks per relevant point		8
(3)	Disadvantages of ZBB		
	2 marks per relevant point		8
			25

Suggested solution

Dear Sally,

Thank you for your email. Please find my responses below.

Non-financial measures

Internal processes

Objective: To ensure tests are successfully executed first time.

Spoiled samples will increase cost, are evidence of internal inefficiencies and may ultimately affect customer service by delays and a requirement for additional samples.

Measure: Retesting costs as a percentage of total testing costs compared to a suitable external benchmark (eg medical profession quality standards.) This will gauge the volume and impact of needing to rerun tests.

Innovation and learning

Objective: Have highly trained staff that are up to date with the latest techniques.

This will ensure best practice and the most accurate results in the broadest range of tests.

Measure: Number of staff training days per head. This will help measure the volume (if not necessarily the success of) continuing professional development undertaken by professional staff.

Customer

Objective: To ensure customer receives results within recommended time frame (depending on type of test).

This is important for the Pathology Laboratory as it will help to maximise the success of the patients' subsequent treatment. This is the lab's 'service quality.'

Measure: Reporting time for each type of test, compared to a suitable benchmark (e.g. a private sector laboratory service, or a comparable hospital service elsewhere.) This will help monitor product quality from the patients' perspective.

Participative budgeting

Department managers appear to be involved in the budgeting process as they are required to submit a divisional cost budget to the senior partner.

However, the MD amends each departmental budget without discussing the amendments and it is evident that the department managers do not have any real involvement in the process as they are unable to influence the final budget for the respective division.

This is likely to have an adverse effect on department managers' motivation, who will feel that they have wasted their time preparing a budget which has effectively been ignored.

As such, department managers are unlikely to feel personally responsible for achieving the target costs bestowed upon them. They may even deliberately fail to achieve the budgeted costs to prove that their own budget was correct and that the amendments imposed by the MD were unrealistic.

Kind regards,

Charlie

Dear Lauren,

Thank you for your email regarding budgeting systems, please find my response to your query outlined below.

Zero based budgeting (ZBB)

ZBB is an approach to budgeting which advocates starting from a zero-base and building the budget/business case for an area of activity from first principles. It is therefore particularly useful in allocating funds to discretionary spend, such as research and development.

From your perspective as Director in the research and development department however, there are several disadvantages to using zero-based budgeting:

Time and skills. The effort and seniority required for the fundamental reassessment of R&D spend is likely to be significant. Specialising in R&D, means that you and your staff may lack the skills and expertise to build a business case for the Department for the coming period.

Motivation. Asking the department to justify their existence and continued employment could well have a damaging impact on morale.

Difficulty forecasting. The nature of R&D is such that it may well be next to impossible to predict the costs and certainly the benefits associated with activity in this area. A lack of identifiable benefits may make it difficult for more senior management to justify investing funds in this area compared to other areas of discretionary spend.

The nature of R&D. R&D requires a creative approach which may be stifled by the need to specify projects. It may be more appropriate to start with the funding available for activity in this area, and work backwards. The starting point may therefore be more appropriately chosen with reference to last years spend, ie an incremental approach.

Should you have any further queries, please don't hesitate to contact me.

Kind regards,

Charlie

Competency coverage

Sub-task	Technical		Business acumen		People		Leadership		Max
1			Balanced scorecard	9					9
2					Participative budgeting	8			8
3					ZBB	8			8
Total				9		16			25

Task 12

Marking scheme

Suggested solution

Dear Ruth,

Please find below my response to your queries.

ROI as a performance measure

Each process division manager is working with equipment that was purchased at different times. As such, the value of the equipment used in ROI calculations is **inconsistent across divisions**. Equipment bought in different years will have been affected by inflation over different timeframes, whilst the number of years of depreciation charged will also be inconsistent.

Head office costs are allocated to divisions and are **beyond the control of the process division** manager. It could be considered unfair to manage the performance of process divisions which include such allocated costs.

Process B determines the input volumes of processes C and D. Processes C and D incur **fixed costs** regardless of the level of output from Process B. As a result, the managers of processes C and D are **unable to control the activity levels** of their respective divisions, which in turn drive divisional profitability.

The profit or loss of each process is influenced by the **transfer prices** that are charged between processes. Transfer prices are based on the budgets of the supplier plus a percentage mark-up. Therefore, the customer's performance will be affected by the **budget of the supplier**. This is unfair as the customer has no control over the supplier's budget.

Transfer pricing

Currently, the transfer price from process B to processes C and D is based on budgeted costs plus a mark-up of 15%. This policy is successful in **rewarding the manager of process B for any efficiencies** that are achieved as well as **protecting processes C and D against any inefficiencies** of Process B. Managers are able to discuss the basis of apportionment of the joint costs.

Process D is able to buy equivalent material from an external supplier at $7.50 per litre which is significantly cheaper than the $9.20 per litre it pays to Process B under the current arrangement. There is clearly a **conflict of interest** here.

Process B produces two joint products, and it is not possible to produce output for Process C without also producing output for Process D. If Process D were to purchase materials from an external supplier, the **output of D from process B would have to be scrapped**. There would be no change to the costs of Process B whilst **external costs incurred by Beauty Co would increase**.

To avoid such a scenario, it is likely that the **transfer price will have to be changed so that process D is no better off from purchasing materials from an external supplier**. This could be achieved by changing the basis on which the joint costs are allocated or by using $7.50 (market price) as the transfer price. It is likely that these changes will alter the profitability of Process B and Process D and consequently the **ROI of each process would also change**.

Costing - traditional approach

Traditional costing systems, notably **absorption costing, assume** that all products **consume resources in proportion to their production volumes**. While this may be true for overheads such as power costs, it does not necessarily hold for all overheads, or an increasing proportion of them, especially those connected with support services.

The amount of **overhead allocated** to individual products by absorption costing therefore bears **very little resemblance** to the **amount of overhead actually incurred** by the products and hence gives management **minimal understanding of the behaviour of overhead costs and**, consequently, they have a lack of **ability to control/reduce them**.

ABC/ABM approach

Activity based costing (**ABC**) attempts to overcome this problem by identifying the activities or transactions (**cost drivers**) which underlie an organisation's activities and which cause the incidence of the activity, and hence the cost of the activity (overheads) to increase. Costs can then be attributed to products according to the number of cost drivers they cause/consume using cost driver rates.

Activity based management (ABM) is the term given to those **management processes that use the information provided by an activity-based cost analysis to improve organisational profitability.**

ABM and cost reduction

Because ABM analyses costs on the basis of what causes them, rather than on the basis of type of expense/cost centre, it provides management with vital information on why costs are being incurred. If management can **reduce the incidence of the cost driver, they can reduce the associated cost.**

ABM involves a variety of **cost reduction techniques.**

(a)   Ensuring activities are performed as efficiently as possible

(b)   Controlling, reducing or eliminating the need to perform activities that do not add value for customers

(c)   Minimising cost drivers

(d)   Improving the design of products

In short, it aims to **ensure that customer needs are met while fewer demands are made on organisational resources.**

Should you have any further questions please don't hesitate to contact me.

Kind regards,

Hilda

Competency coverage

Sub-task	Technical		Business acumen		People		Leadership		Max
1			Performance measures	8					8
2							Transfer pricing	8	8
3			ABM and cost reduction	9					9
Total				17				8	25

Topic 5 – E2 Task Practice

The Practice Tasks that follow are intended to serve several purposes:

- They are spread across the key topics in the syllabus, to enable you to recap important areas of technical knowledge

- Although not based on the real preseen they have been designed to reflect the style of the Tasks in the ICS Exam, so that you can use them to develop your ICS Exam Technique

- Note that as they are not based on a separate preseen, they contain more background/scenario information than you would expect in the 'unseen' Tasks in your real exam.

- The solutions are intended to be "student achievable" and reflective of the level of detail CIMA provide in their Examiners Solutions.

- They should provide you with a good range of business situations that could be applied to the real preseen. As well as attempting each Practice Task in its own right, you should also take some to reflect afterwards as to how the issues you've worked through could relate to the real preseen organisation.

Topic 5 – E2 Primary Tasks

Task 13 – RM Company

Indicative timing: 45 minutes (excluding Background Information)

Background information:

Fiona Mason is the Chief Executive of RM Company, a manufacturer of ready-made meals.

You work as a management consultant for G Consulting, which has been hired by Fiona to assist with a situation at RM Company.

Extract of a telephone conversation between yourself and Fiona

> **Fiona:** Many thanks for taking this on. It is imperative that my business finds a way to move forward.
>
> **You:** It would be useful if you could outline the current situation as you see it. I understand that the company is facing difficult business conditions.
>
> **Fiona:** We know this is as a result of strong competition from supermarket own brand products and seemingly endless consumer demand for variety and new products. I appreciate that the company needs to improve its performance in bringing new products to market. However, the company currently faces several problems because our new product development (NPD) process is not as good as it should be. For example, collaboration between departments is essential to successful NPD, but in the past the NPD process has resulted in disagreements and arguments between the various departments.
>
> **You:** Are there specific departments or disagreements that my work should focus on?
>
> **Fiona:** The Marketing Department complain that the Research and Development (R&D) Department is very slow in responding to their proposals for new recipes and the whole process of R&D takes too long. The Production Department complains that R&D does not consider the implications for the production process when coming up with new recipes and product packaging. The sales team is frustrated with the length of time the whole NPD process takes. It says that the lack of new products puts it at a disadvantage when negotiating with retailers to sell RM Company's products.
>
> **You:** What position does your Finance Department take in all these arguments?
>
> **Fiona:** The Finance Department is concerned that the investment in NPD does not provide adequate returns, and both the Marketing and R&D Departments are always over budget. However, the other departments see Finance as controlling rather than supporting new product development. So as you can see, we are in something of a difficult situation and I don't really understand how the business has ended up in this state.

Task

You have just received this email from Fiona

From:	Fiona FionaM@RMCo.co.uk
Sent:	30th June 20X5, 18:47
Subject:	A troubled work environment

Thank you for taking the time to discuss the current situation at RM Company with me last week.

Following our telephone conversation, I have decided to establish a cross-functional team to work on a new range of luxury ready-made meals designed to appeal to the sophisticated end of the market. I have appointed Thomas as head of a new cross-functional NPD projects team and given him the particular remit of leading and managing the NPD team. Thomas has never led a cross-functional team before so I need your help in this as well.

Please can you assist me by preparing briefing notes on the following:

- Identify the nature of the conflict we are experiencing at RM Company. I need to understand why it is occurring, and, what its sources are. This analysis will be very useful in helping us resolve the issue.

- Prepare notes I can discuss with Thomas to recommend the sorts of things he should do to be effective in leading and managing the new NPD project team.

Many thanks.

Kind regards,

Fiona

Chief Executive
RM Co.
E: FionaM@RMCo.co.uk

Write your response to Fiona

Task 14 – F Company

Indicative timing: 45 minutes (excluding Background Information)

Background information:

F Company is a medium sized business that manufactures electrical kitchen appliances including food processors, toasters, juicers and coffee makers. You are the company's management accountant.

Extract from management meeting minutes for Company F

Gillian Salcombe – Managing Director

"Good morning everyone. As we all know, in the last twelve months we have lost market share to our competitors and have underperformed on most of our key performance indicators. Our future survival is threatened as new entrants are stealing market share and our customers are increasingly demanding new products and enhanced design features.

I think it is fair to say that we have been too complacent, we haven't responded well to the changing environmental conditions and our strategic planning process is non-existent. I am also quite concerned about what I have been hearing about different areas of the company pursuing conflicting objectives.

I propose that a more formal, top-down approach to developing business strategy be adopted. This will enable us to react to developments taking place in the external environment, and should help us promote goal congruence."

Peter Chard – HR Director

"I have to say, Gillian, I strongly disagree. We clearly operate in a dynamic environment and that means that adopting a formal approach to developing strategy is a waste of our time and resources. I really think that we can achieve sustainable competitive advantage by making the most of our unique combination of resources, skills and capabilities. "

Task

A few days ago you had a visit from Melplash Bay, a newly recruited Business Development Director with a marketing background.

You have just received the following email from Melplash:

From:	Melplash Melplash@FCompany.co.uk
Sent:	12th October 20X4
Subject:	Re: Benefits and drawbacks of the top-down approach to setting strategy

I am confused about the difference of opinion between Gillian and Peter and want to know who – if anyone – is correct. I'm sure they were using the terminology 'resource-based view' and 'positioning view' when they were talking the other day but I do not know what these terms mean. I'm wondering whether we can put this information to good use somehow to make certain our position in the market place and gain competitive advantage.

I would like to you to produce briefing notes to cover the following points:

- Explain the benefits and drawbacks associated with F Company adopting a top down approach to the formulation of business strategy.

- Compare and contrast both Gillian and Peter's views on strategic development. Please email me your thoughts on this by the end of the day.

Kind regards,

Melplash Bay

Business Development Director
F Company
E: Melplash@FCompany.co.uk

Write your response to Melplash

Task 15 – COL project

Indicative timing: 45 minutes (excluding Background Information)

Background information:

You are an assistant project technician at SYS, a local systems development company, working under David, a project manager. The date is March 30th 20X6.

SYS has accepted a project to upgrade the systems at COL, a private education college. David thinks that the COL project seems like a perfect opportunity for you to step up and demonstrate the project management skills you have acquired to date.

Extract of the project brief

Notes – COL

– Private college offering online tuition and qualifications to candidates all over the world

– Board of Directors has decided to upgrade its computer system. This is to enable COL to offer <u>faster</u>, <u>more flexible</u> delivery of courses and examination materials.

– COL facing increasing competition in the delivery of online tuition and qualifications from both private and public colleges throughout the world.

– Clear objectives for the system are in place but COL cannot manage the project for themselves due to lack of expertise

– The Project Manager is responsible for:

1. All of the key stages of the project management process, including the project plan

2. Leading the project team, made up of mainly SYS designers and also a number of IT staff and users from COL.

3. Communication of the project's progress and events to Mrs Yolo, the senior IT manager at COL

– Budget $3m. Overruns borne by SYS!

– Deadline 30th March 20X7

– Data security is paramount – unauthorised access (to candidate details including results) seem to be biggest risk

– Close collaboration with staff at COL is really very important

– Mrs Yolo needs to be managed carefully – take care to communicate frequently with her and her team.

Task

David calls you into his office.

"Ah, there you are. I am currently extremely busy and need you to construct an outline project plan for the upgrade of COL's online system for my presentation to the key stakeholders of the project.

I am also in the process of putting together an information pack for some new joiners at SYS who are having their induction next week. I am trying to think of some points to include regarding the skills of the project manager and I am a little bit stuck.

I would like you to imagine for a moment that you were the project manager on the COL project, recommend the main skills that you would require to lead the project team. I know I'm putting you on the spot a bit but I'm sure you've got some ideas

By the end of the day, please can you provide me with briefing notes on these two points:

- An outline project plan for COL
- Recommendations on the main project management skills needed to lead the COL project."

Write your response to David

Task 16 – The Heritage Trust

Indicative timing: 45 minutes (excluding Background Information)

Background information:

The Heritage Trust is a charity which was founded in 1830 with the aim of acquiring buildings of national interest and preserving them for the public to visit, along with the art collections and antiques within them. The Trust now owns over 200 houses nationwide, many of which also have large gardens.

Historically, about 30% of the Trust's income has come from government grants, reflecting the importance the Government attaches to preserving the nation's heritage. About 50% of the Trust's total income comes from membership fees. (Members pay an annual subscription which then allows them free entry to any of the Trust's properties.) The remaining 20% comes from a combination of admission charges (which non-members pay to visit the properties) and sales in the gift shops and restaurants which many properties have.

The income is used for the continued preservation of the properties and their art collections, as well as paying for the administrative costs of the Trust, including staff costs. Each property has a salaried manager, who lives on site, although a number of volunteers also help with the upkeep of the properties.

The Trust is governed by a Board of Trustees, who are well-known and respected figures in the field of heritage and the arts. The Trust's strategy is developed by the Director General, Benjamin Batty in conjunction with the Trustees.

The Board of Trustees and Benjamin Batty have always believed that there are a number of 'flagship' properties which people want to preserve and support. These properties encourage people to become members of the Trust and to renew their memberships each year, regardless of whether they actually visit the properties.

In the annual budget, a share of the central membership income is allocated to each individual property. The amount each property receives depends on whether or not it is a 'flagship' property, and how important the collections within the property are believed to be.

Being the manager of a 'flagship' property is considered an important position and they enjoy many privileges, including spacious private accommodation within the property itself, and a dedicated personal assistant.

You are the management accountant at the Heritage Trust. Two months ago all employees of the trust received an internal memo informing the trust of the government's plan to half the annual grant to the Trust and Benjamin Batty's subsequent decision to resign

Following this announcement, the Trust appointed a new Director General from the private sector to develop a new business strategy. The new Director General, Christopher Cross, was appointed to give the Trust the best possible chance at increasing its income from commercial activities rather than making significant changes to operations. Christopher was previously the CEO of a major retail chain.

Task

Christopher has produced a strategic planning document, and circulated it to managers across the organisation. An extract of this has been presented below (Exhibit 1).

Exhibit 1

- In future, the central budget will be allocated to properties according to visitor popularity. This is designed to stimulate properties to come up with interesting and innovative ideas to increase visitor numbers.

- Removing the property managers' personal assistants, and giving them IT training where necessary so that they can do their own administration

- Recruiting five regional business development managers to increase commercial income by selling a wider range of souvenirs from the gift shops, and hosting open air concerts and theatre productions in the grounds of the properties

- Recruit an e-commerce business manager to develop an online store

A few days, later, Christopher calls you into his office and says the following:

"Thanks for coming by. To get straight to the point, it seems that my plans have caused some consternation. The managers of the 'flagship' properties seem rather quite angry. My proposal to link budgets to visitor numbers has been particularly poorly received. Some people are even saying I'm under-valuing the historical significance of our properties in a search for popularity! And if that wasn't enough, they've been lobbying the trustees behind my back, and talking to TV stations! It's been a complete nightmare!

I'm afraid I didn't have much time to carry out a full consultation before coming up with the proposals but running the Trust isn't that different to running a retail chain! After all, it's not as though I'm meddling with the Trust's culture and values…to be honest I'm at a bit of a loss.

I was hoping that with your experience with Benjamin Batty, you'd be able to explain to me a bit about where I went wrong.

Please prepare for me a memorandum which:

- Analyses the underlying cultural issues that have led to the resistance I am currently experiencing.

- Recommends appropriate steps that could be taken to overcome the resistance to my proposals'

Thanks."

Write your response to Christopher

Task 17 – The DE Company

Indicative timing: 45 minutes (excluding Background Information)

Background information:

The DE Company has two operational divisions, Division D and Division E. You are the accounts assistant at The DE Company.

Jillian Leeds is your line manager, the company's management accountant. During a recent conversation Jillian explained her frustration about maintaining both the Accounts Payable team and the Payroll team in the UK. She feels the decision to not outsource these functions is inefficient and costly.

Extract of divisional performance numbers

The following statement shows the performance of each division for the year ended 30 April 20X5:

	D $'000	E $'000
Sales	500,200	201,600
Variable cost	380,400	140,000
Contribution	119,800	61,600
Fixed costs	30,000	20,000
Operating profit	89,800	41,600

Notes:

1. Division E manufactures just one type of component. It sells the components to external customers and also to Division D.

2. Production Capacity:

   Division E – 140,000 units

   Division D – 35,000 units

3. Demand (Number of units):

Internal		External	
E	D	E	D
70,000	N/A	112,000	35,000

4. External customers buy from Division E at the current price of $1,550 per unit.

   The current policy of The DE Company is that internal sales should be transferred at their opportunity cost. Consequently during the year, some components were transferred to Division D at the market price and some were transferred at variable cost.

Task

You receive the following email from the management accountant.

From:	Jillian Leeds jilee@DECompany.co.uk
Sent:	3rd May 20X5, 11:27
Subject:	Divisional Performance

This transfer pricing situation has been frustrating me for a long time but has never made it to the top of my priority list. I thought it would be good to get you involved as it's something new and exciting, and it helps the business.

In addition to this, I need your help with my latest project. The senior management team are currently exploring the possibility of outsourcing the Accounts Payable and Payroll functions to a third party outsourcer based in an Eastern European country. This would be our first outsourcing project, so we currently have no experience of negotiating this level of change in the company.

So, please can you write a report which includes the following:

- A discussion of the effect of possible changes in external demand on the profits of Division E, assuming the current transfer pricing policy continues. Basic supporting calculations would of course be helpful, as would a discussion of the appropriateness of the current transfer pricing policy from the perspective of EACH of the divisional managers AND the company as a whole.

- An explanation of how we should approach any negotiations with the trade unions (which represent those employees currently working in the Accounts Payable and Payroll functions) and the prospective outsourcer.

Any questions that arise, please get in touch.

Kind regards,

Jill

Management Accountant
DE Company
E: jilee@DECompany.co.uk

Write your response to Jillian

Task 18 – A2G Advertising Agency

Indicative timing: 45 minutes (excluding Background Information)

Background information:

A2G Advertising Agency currently employs a range of specialist staff in order to be able to develop promotional campaigns for its clients. The agency currently undertakes all of the creative work involved in developing campaigns, as well as the business side of running a successful advertising agency. This includes buying advertisement slots on TV and advertising space in newspapers and magazines.

You work for SC Consulting and you have been hired as a consultant by A2G which is currently experiencing some problems. Yesterday, you attended a meeting with A2G's CEO, Eleanor Tall. Eleanor explained the problems A2G is facing. During this meeting you made the following notes.

Extract of notes from the A2G meeting

A number of key members of the agency's creative team have recently resigned and the agency is finding it difficult to replace them.

A2G is experiencing rising costs associated with running a sophisticated graphic design studio and state-of-the-art TV and film production facilities.

Creative processes are seen as the company's Critical Success Factor. Creative staff are supported by graphic designers and producers.

A2G is seen as a mid-level agency i.e., not the most innovative or cutting edge, but the quality of output is consistently good.

Pricing is a problem because costs are rising but the industry is highly competitive so prices have been kept at 20X5 levels.

Task

After the meeting you received the following email.

From:	Eleanor Tall <TallE@A2G.com>
Sent:	13th September 20X7
Subject:	Transaction Cost Theory, and the Resource-based and Positioning Views

To address the issues we discussed yesterday the owners of A2G have been exploring something called Transaction Cost Theory. Some of the owners are interested in the possibility of outsourcing some activities that are presently undertaken in-house at A2G. Although, on the face of it, A2G would be able to operate from smaller premises with fewer staff, the owners are speculating on whether or not outsourcing would be the right decision financially.

Furthermore, I recently attended a conference run by the local Chamber of Commerce. During the keynote speakers presentation he referred to the different approaches to strategic development that businesses may adopt. He mentioned the use of a 'resource-based' and 'positioning' approach.

During this challenging time for A2G the owners are keen to explore all options for improving business performance. As a result they have asked you to provide them with some detail on Business Process Re-engineering (BPR).

Please could you provide me with a memorandum which explains:

- How Transaction Cost Theory could assist the owners of A2G to decide which activities it could outsource.

- Relatively briefly, whether a 'resource-based' or 'positioning' approach to strategic development would be the most appropriate for A2G.

- How BPR could be applied to any processes kept in-house at A2G

Many thanks,

Eleanor Tall
Chief Executive
A2G

E: TallE@A2G.com

Write your response to Eleanor

Topic 5 – E2 Primary Tasks Solutions

Task 13

Marking scheme

	Marks
Sub-task 1 – Nature and sources of conflict	
Up to 2 marks per relevant well explained point:	Up to 2 each
Explanation of horizontal conflict	
Pressure caused by business conditions	
Task interdependence	
Personality types	
Incompatibility of goals	
Other sensible suggestions	
Maximum for sub-task 1	<u>10</u>
Sub-task 2 – Managing and leading a new team	
Up to 2 marks per relevant well explained point:	Up to 2 each
Explanation of negotiation	
Individuals	
The group	
Leadership	
Participation in decision making	
Delegation	
Communication	
Team meetings	
Maximum for sub-task 2	<u>15</u>
MAXIMUM FOR TASK	<u>25</u>

Suggested solution

Briefing note

To: Fiona FionaM@RMCo.co.uk
Date: 2nd July 20X5, 13:02
Subject: A troubled work environment

Introduction

This briefing note sets out the information that you requested in relation to the nature and sources of the conflict being experienced at RM Company and considerations for Thomas managing and leading a new team.

(1) **Sources of conflict**

RM Company is suffering the effects of **horizontal conflict**, since the conflicts are arising between groups and individuals that do not have a hierarchical relationship and are of more or less equal status in the company.

The various disputes have occurred for several reasons.

Incompatibility of goals

The primary goals of the various departments involved, are themselves effectively incompatible. For example, the R&D department appear slow but maybe striving for technical excellence, while the anxiety of the sales department may reflect goals of continuing growth.

Incompatibility of personalities in different business functions

People working in different functions tend to have rather different personal priorities, interests, attitudes and values.

Task interdependence

It is necessary for all the departments to co-operate closely if successful NPD is to take place. Any lack of co-operation from any department is likely to produce significant frustration and further conflict.

Work pressure

RM Company is facing difficult business conditions, which are likely to produce stress effects all responsible members of staff, both because of awareness of the need for improved performance and as a result of pressure from the board.

(2) **Managing and leading a new team**

The task of developing a new team might be considered under three headings:

<u>The individuals</u>

Thomas must ensure that the members of the new project, between them, possess the skills, experience and aptitudes necessary to develop successfully this new range of luxury foods. Past disputes mean that perhaps the most important personal quality the team members will require is the **commitment to working productively together**.

Belbin suggests that the effective functioning of a team depends on the ability of the members to play a range of important team roles. These roles are co-ordinator, shaper, implementer, monitor-evaluator, resource investigator, team worker, specialist and completer/finisher.

<u>The group</u>

New teams develop and mature over time, finding ways to operate and relate. Thomas could look to build the team by controlling and accelerating this process. The development process was described by *Tuckman* as taking place in four stages.

Forming is the process of bringing the group together and beginning to work out its aims, structure and processes. The 'getting to know each other' process should be encouraged here since team members come from different functions and may not even know each other.

Storming is a period of open conflict between members about objectives, methods and relationships during which priorities and roles emerge. It should lead to a robust basis for co-operation in the future.

Norming is a period of settling down with the development of group norms about work requirements and methods and social expectations. Thomas may need to encourage 'overarching' norms and goals in order to overcome inter-functional differences.

Performing productive work follows as the final phase, when the team is ready to collaborate on efficient task performance.

Leadership

The NPD project team will include experienced professionals with their own competences and expectations. An autocratic leadership style is unlikely to be the most productive when working with such people. The **maturity** of the team, in *Hersey and Blanchard's* terms, needs to be considered. Maturity of a team is defined as:

(i)   A desire for achievement
(ii)   The willingness and ability to accept responsibility
(iii)   Education, experience or skills relevant to the particular task

Thomas must map his style (for example delegating) to the maturity of the team.

In the newly formed cross-functional team it is likely that the maturity of the team will be high, given the functional skills and experience of the team members. Thomas should therefore adopt a leadership style with a low degree of directive behaviour. **Participation in decision-making** and a high degree of **delegation** will be important and will help maximise the potential synergy of cross-functional working by drawing on each stakeholder's areas of expertise.

The complexity of the task and the need for a wide range of co-ordinated inputs will make **communication** very important. Thomas must provide clear objectives and decisions, provide briefings on future activity and give feedback on the project progress. Thomas must also ensure that the team members communicate effectively with each other. This could be achieved by holding regular **meetings** held at suitable intervals to ensure that important matters are not overlooked and there is general understanding of work and progress.

Should you have any queries on the above, please do not hesitate to contact me.

Competency coverage

Sub Task	Technical		Business acumen		People		Leadership		Integration		Max
1					Nature and sources of conflict	10					10
2							Managing and leading a new team	15			15
Total						10		15			25

Task 14

Marking scheme

Marks

Sub-task 1 – The top-down approach
Up to 2 marks per relevant well explained point: Up to 2 each
Benefits:
Long term view
Structured approach
Goal congruence
Improved control
Set by experienced staff
Used because it works

Drawbacks:
Lack of flexibility
Lack of innovation
Expense
Implementation of ideas
Lack of motivation
Strategy setting is not a rational process
Maximum for sub-task 1 <u>12</u>

Sub-task 2 – Resource based and positioning views
Up to 2 marks per relevant well explained point: Up to 2 each
Sustainability of competitive advantage
Flexibility of company in order to respond to changing environments
Outsourcing
Focus on a particular market segment
Possession of scarce resources
Core competencies
Other relevant points
Maximum for sub-task 2 <u>13</u>
MAXIMUM FOR TASK <u>25</u>

Suggested solution

Briefing note

To: Melplash Melplash@FCompany.co.uk
Date: 9th October 20X4, 18:44
Subject: Top-down approach and contrasting views to setting strategy

Introduction

This briefing note sets out the information that you requested in relation to the benefits and drawbacks of the top-down approach for A2G and compares the directors contrasting views of strategic development for A2G.

(1) Top-down planning for F Company

The most comprehensive kind of formal, top down strategic planning is described by the **rational model** of strategic analysis, strategic choice and strategy implementation.

Benefits

The board is particularly concerned about **developments in its immediate market environment**, having lost market share. Continuing comprehensive, ongoing **environmental analysis** should be one of the most important features, therefore, of any system of planning introduced by the company. This would be a fundamental aspect of the rational model.

Further benefits include:

- It helps the organisation to take a **long view** and encourages **suppliers and employees** to think in terms of a long-term relationship.

- It guides the **allocation of resources by** setting a standard by which the actual performance of the organisation is **measured and controlled**.

- It **co-ordinates the activities** of the various parts of the organisation, ensuring the integration of operational management decisions into the higher strategy, the wider organisational context and longer term goals. This is another particular concern the board has at F Company.

Drawbacks

The concept of formal processes for strategy generation and their limited success in practice has led to criticisms of both the rational model and the very idea of strategic planning as a separate business activity.

- The formal approach encourages a sense of **omniscience and control** among planners: this is dangerous because of the **inherent unpredictability of the business environment**

- Environmental uncertainty also tends to lead managers to adopt an approach of **bounded rationality**, satisfying themselves with solutions that are acceptable rather than ideal.

- There is an associated problem of **detachment**: planners' tendency to assume that strategy can be divorced from operations. This is inappropriate. Planners rarely have to implement the strategies they devise and feedback occurs too late or is badly filtered.

- The formal approach is usually couched in terms of a **planning cycle** and this may extend for up to five years. Even a one year cycle is not responsive enough to changing circumstances.

- The **expense and complexity** of the formal approach are inappropriate for smaller businesses.

(2) Resource based vs positioning approach

Positioning approach

The views of Gillian and Peter represent opposite sides in a current debate about the best way to approach strategy. Gillian believes the positioning approach is best for Company F, whereas Peter believes they should be following a resource-based approach. The rational model is only one of several approaches to a strategic method that is based on the process of **adapting the organisation to its environment**. This adaptive or **positioning-based strategy** approach pays great attention to markets, consumers and competitors, and may be contrasted with the **resource-based approach**.

Arguments against the positioning-view include:

- In many modern industries, the **rate of environmental change is too great** for effective positioning strategies to be developed.

- **Positioning advantages cannot be sustained in the long term**. Advantageous product market positions are **too easy to copy** to last long and more rapid product lifecycles erode initial advantage.

- It is more difficult to **adapt the organisation** than to **adopt a new environment**. The positioning approach may require significant change within the firm, which is difficult to achieve.

Resource based approach

The resource based approach to strategy emphasises the **possession of scarce resources** and **core competences** by the organisation. Strategy, it is suggested, consists of exploiting such resources and core competences in order to gain competitive advantage. This approach lies behind the growing practice of **outsourcing**: the organisation concentrates its efforts on those parts of its operations that no other organisation can perform on its behalf.

Competences must therefore be developed and kept up to date on a continuing basis. *Johnson and Scholes* define core competences as those that both **outperform competitors** and are **difficult to imitate**.

The resource-based approach is not without its difficulties.

- Core competences are **difficult to identify and assess**: a wrong appraisal could lead to the loss of wider competence or source of advantage by misdirected outsourcing.

- Attempts to apply core competences (or other resources) widely across a range of markets and operations may make the firm **vulnerable to more focused, single market operations**.

- The emphasis on unique resources is reminiscent of the 'product orientation' decried by marketing experts: competitors who are more in touch with **market requirements** may be more successful. On the other hand, a strategy based on a sequence of unique products, as in the pharmaceutical industry, can be successful.

Competency coverage

Sub Task	Technical		Business acumen		People		Leadership		Integration		Max
1			Benefits and drawbacks of the top-down approach to strategy	12							12
2			Resource based and positioning views	13							13
Total				25							25

Task 15

Marking scheme

Sub-task 1 – Project plan
Up to 2 marks per relevant well explained point: Up to 2 each

Project Manager
Project Team
Business need for project
Communication and reporting
Resources
Budgets
Risks
Change Management
Other relevant points
Maximum for sub-task 1   <u>13</u>

Sub-task 2 – Project manager skills
Up to 2 marks per relevant well explained point: Up to 2 each
Leadership
Organisational
Communication
Change management
Personal Qualities
Other relevant points
Maximum for sub-task 2   <u>12</u>
MAXIMUM FOR TASK   <u>25</u>

Suggested solution

Briefing note

To: David
Date: 31st March 20X6
Subject: COL project

Introduction

This briefing note sets out the information that you requested regarding the outline project plan and an overview of the recommended project management skills for the COL project.

(1)   **Outline Project Plan**

Project Name: Upgrade of COL on-line course delivery system project

Project Manager: The project manager is David. David is responsible for all of the key stages of the project management process. He is responsible for leading the project team.

Project Team: The project team consists of SYS designers, COL IT staff and users from COL.

Purpose/ Business Need: To update the online course delivery to meet the objectives set out by the Board of Directors and senior managers of COL.

Deliverables: The project must be delivered within 12 months at a cost of no more than $3 million.

Communication and Reporting: The project manager, David, will communicate with and report to Mrs Yolo, the senior IT manager at COL. This section of the plan would include how plans will be communicated to members of the team, the nature and timing of meetings and reports, as well as details of how other stakeholders will be kept informed of project progress.

Technical Plan: This section of the plan would include the technical features of the project, such as system specifications, systems diagrams, and so on.

Project schedule: This may include Gantt charts or network diagrams and will describe the main phases of the project and key milestones. A work breakdown structure will need to be provided to the project team to identify all of the tasks and those responsible for them.

Resources: The resources required for successful implementation of the project would be listed here. Resources should be identified for all key activities and a resource histogram may be used to show resource requirements.

Budgets: A detailed budget and cash flow forecast would be required. There is no overrun allowed in the project from the original budget of $3 million. Any overrun will be borne by SYS.

Risk: Risks should be identified, assessed and where possible quantified. One of the main enhancements to the updated system required by COL is the security of candidates' details.

Change management: Requests for changes to this plan may be initiated by either SYS or COL, represented by Mrs Yolo and David respectively. All change requests will be reviewed and approved or rejected by the project board.

Post-implementation audit: The final project will be reviewed post-implementation to evaluate its success and as an aid to future projects.

(2) **Recommended project management skills**

The project manager would need a range of skills to manage the COL project, including the following:

- Leadership and delegation skills

    The project manager of the COL project would need to adopt an appropriate leadership style. A participatory style of leadership is likely to be appropriate for the project to upgrade COL's systems. However, an autocratic decisive style may be required on occasions. In this situation tasks need to be delegated appropriately. This may be a particularly delicate task as some of the project team are not SYS employees. It is recommended that project team members are empowered to take responsibility for certain tasks. This should help to avoid the project manager taking on too much of the workload.

- Organisational skills

    The project manager would need good organisational skills to manage the various project tasks and associated project paperwork. All project documentation must be clear and distributed to all who require it. Appropriate project management tools should be used to analyse and monitor the projects progress.

- Communication and negotiation skills

  Strong communication skills are required because of the need to communicate formally with COL (per the project plan) and the need to communicate informally with all stakeholders involved. This will involve listening to project team members as well as other stakeholders. The project manager will likely need to be able to persuade reluctant team members or stakeholders to support the project. This means they may need to negotiate on staffing and other resources, quality and disputes.

- Change control and management skills

  Changes in any project are inevitable. Changes to this project could arise from a variety of sources and have the potential to disrupt the progress of the project. The project manager must be able to minimise the effects of these on the quality, time and cost of the project, especially given the one year period to complete the project and the limited project budget.

- Personal qualities

  In addition to the project management skills discussed it is recommended that the project manager possesses the following personal qualities:

  Flexibility, as circumstances may develop which require a change in the plan.

  Creativity, if one method of completing a task proves impractical then a new approach may be required.

  Technical skills, in order to gain customer confidence the project manager would have to demonstrate technical competence even though they will not directly carrying out the activities of the project.

Competency coverage

Sub Task	Technical		Business acumen		People		Leadership		Integration		Max
1			Project plan	13							13
2							Project manager skills	12			12
Total				13					12		25

Task 16

Marking scheme

	Marks
Sub-task 1 – Cultural issues	
Up to 2 marks per relevant well explained point:	Up to 2 each
Use of a suitable cultural model such as	
Johnson's Cultural web	
McKinsey's 7S Framework	
Maximum for sub-task 1	**15**
Sub-task 2 – Overcoming resistance	
Up to 2 marks per relevant well explained point:	Up to 2 each
Communication	
Education	
Consultation	
Negotiation	
Manipulation	
Maximum for sub-task 2	**10**
MAXIMUM FOR TASK	**25**

Suggested solution

MEMORANDUM

To: Christopher Cross
Date: Thursday 12 June 20X6
Subject: Cultural issues and overcoming resistance

Introduction

This memorandum considers the cultural issues being faced, and how to overcome them.

(1) **Cultural Issues**

The Trust's culture can be assessed by looking at its **cultural web**, and from this we can identify some underlying issues which have caused your plans to be resisted.

Symbols are the **representations of an organisation's culture**

At the Trust, symbols such as the **accommodation** and **personal assistants** for the managers at the flagship properties indicate that these people are considered very important.

Threats to status – The proposal to **remove the managers' personal assistants** would have involved removing a key status symbol, and would therefore have been very unpopular with the flagship managers.

The **power structures** of an organisation reflect who has the real power in an organisation, and who has the greatest influence on decisions and the strategic direction of that organisation.

The Trustees appear to realise the need for change, but the flagship managers are likely to be more hostile, recognising that the need for a more commercial focus could jeopardise the privileges they earn, without seemingly having to do very much to justify them.

The **control systems** of an organisation concern the way it is controlled. They include financial systems, quality systems and rewards. The budgets at the Trust again reflect the **dominance and importance given to the flagship properties**, and art or antique collections of historical merit. In effect, the system seems designed to **reinforce the importance and prestige of the flagship properties**.

Rituals and Routines such as the behaviour and actions of people in an organisation signal what is considered acceptable behaviour in that organisation.

Perhaps more importantly, the property managers seem to think it is **acceptable for them to write letters to the press and appear on television** to promote their views and gather support in opposition to your plans.

Stories are used by members of the organisation to illustrate the sorts of things it values. In the Trust, the **stories reinforce the impression given by its power structures.** We have already seen that the power structures are directed towards heritage rather than promoting the popularity of the properties with the general public.

(2) **Overcoming Resistance**

Communication plays a vital role in the change management process, and the fact that the Trust's management have been very critical of the lack of consultation throughout the process suggests that the way that you have communicated the changes and the need for change has not been as effective as it could have been.

The managers' resistance could be overcome by a clear communication process, which should include the following steps:

- **Communication**

  As soon as possible, you should explain the need for the changes to the managers, in particular that the reduction in government grants means that the Trust needs to increase the income it generates from its own commercial activities.

- **Education**

  In the communication process, you should also explain the aims of your strategy, and how it will address the issues caused by the reduction in government grants. You should also explain how you propose to implement it.

- **Consultation**

  However, it is important that the managers are not simply told what the strategy is and how it will be implemented, but that they are consulted about it.

- **Negotiation**

  Despite the communication and consultation process, there will inevitably still be some managers who still feel aggrieved by the changes, and by their loss of status. The Trust may need to make some concessions to encourage them to accept the changes.

- **Manipulation**

  The Trust may also need to manipulate some managers by appealing to their better nature and asking them to set aside their personal ambition for the good of the Trust as a whole.

Competency coverage

Sub Task	Technical		Business acumen		People		Leadership		Integration		Max
1					Cultural issues	15					15
2							Overcoming resistance	10			10
Total						15		10			25

Task 17

Marking scheme

	Marks
Sub-task 1 – Transfer pricing	
Up to 2 marks per relevant well explained point:	Up to 2 each
Effects of change in external demand on profit	
Supporting calculations	
Appropriateness of current transfer pricing policy:	
From perspective of Manager of Division D	
From perspective of Manager of Division E	
From perspective of company as a whole	
Maximum for sub-task 1	**10**
Sub-task 2 – Negotiation	
Up to 2 marks per relevant well explained point:	Up to 2 each
Explanation of negotiation	
Preparation for the negotiation	
Conducting the negotiation	
Closing the negotiation	
Other relevant points	
Maximum for sub-task 2	12
Integration	3
MAXIMUM FOR TASK	25

Suggested solution

Report

To: Jillian Leeds jilee@DECompany.co.uk
Date: 4th May 20X5
Subject: Divisional Performance

Introduction

This report sets out the information that you requested in relation to the current and proposed transfer pricing policy between Division D and Division E and considerations for negotiating the outsourcing of the Accounts Payable and the Payroll functions.

(1) **The effect of possible changes in external demand on the profits of Division E**

Division E has sold 28,000 units to Division D **without making any profit on these units**. The market value of these is $43.4 million which is $15.4 million higher than the **transfer price** (28,000 units × $1,000 per unit = $28.0 million).

Although charging the full market value price may not be appropriate for Division D as the units could not be sold externally, there should be some **reward accruing to Division E** for the supply of the components.

A **transfer price above variable cost** would reduce the profits of Division D and increase the profits of Division E by the same amount. An **increase in external demand** would mean more components supplied to Division D would be at **market value** which would further increase the profits of Division E and lower the profits of Division D.

The impact of the Transfer Pricing Policy on the parties involved

Division D

Division D is operating at capacity so the company is not wasting resources here and the manager of Division D should be reasonably content as he is able to satisfy external demand for his product.

He may however be frustrated at paying "opportunity cost" price for the component he buys internally. He is effectively paying more for the transferred components than he might need to, simply because there is excess external demand for Division E's product.

Division E

Division E is currently operating at capacity however there is unsatisfied demand for their product therefore they are likely to be resentful about having to transfer components internally.

Making the transfers at opportunity cost is a sensible way of highlighting the impact of the transfer and ensuring that the selling division (E) does not suffer a loss of profitability, however if there is unsatisfied external demand, there is a loss of actual realised profit as discussed above.

Company perspective

The managers' frustration could have a knock-on impact on things like motivation and staff turnover, both of which ultimately impact profitability.

The company could establish whether there is a supplier of the component that could supply Division D and free up capacity for Division E to supply its external customers. It is essential to ensure it is cost effective to supply Division D externally.

(2) **Negotiation**

Negotiation is a process whereby two parties come together to confer with a view to concluding a jointly acceptable agreement.

The process involves two main elements:

Purposeful persuasion: whereby each party attempts to persuade the other to accept its case by marshalling arguments, backed by factual information and analysis.

Constructive compromise: whereby both parties accept the need to move closer toward each other's position, identifying the parameters of common ground within and between their positions, where there is room for concessions to be made, while still meeting the needs of both parties.

It is likely that constructive compromise will be needed in the negotiations. DE Company will wish to minimise its costs and maximise the level of service it receives from the outsourcer whereas the outsourcer will wish to maximise its income and minimise the resources it needs to devote to the contract. Similarly, in the trade union negotiations, the trade union will not want to agree to job losses, but it might recognise that they are inevitable and concentrate instead on persuading management to provide generous severance pay above the legal minimum and to consider **redeployment opportunities. Effective negotiation should go through a number of stages:**

Preparation

A framework for the negotiations that the management might use to ensure that the negotiations themselves are effective might 'include':

- Set objectives for the negotiation.
- Gather information on the issues over which negotiations are going to be concluded.
- Identify potential areas of conflict.
- Identify potential areas of movement.
- Formulate a negotiating strategy.

Conducting the negotiation

Some of the considerations around conducting negotiations might include:

- Identifying the common ground.
- Considering new proposals or counter proposals.
- Making concessions.

Closing the negotiation

At the conclusion of negotiations, both parties must be satisfied that all issues have been discussed, and they must understand exactly what has been agreed.

Should further information be required, please get in touch.

Competency coverage

Sub Task	Technical		Business acumen		People		Leadership		Integration		Max
1			Transfer pricing	10							10
2					Negotiation	12					12
Total				10		12				3	25

Task 18

Marking scheme

	Marks
Sub-task 1 – How Transaction Cost Theory (TCT)could be used by A2G	
Up to 2 marks per relevant well explained point:	Up to 2 each
Definition of TCT	
Explanation of core versus non-core activities of A2G	
Recommend how TCT could be used by A2G	
Discuss how TCT could help A2G	
Maximum for sub-task 1	<u>10</u>
Sub-task 2 – Resource based vs positioning based approach	
Up to 2 marks per relevant well explained point:	Up to 2 each
Definition of resource-based view	
Definition of positioning view	
Comparison of the resource-based and positioning view	
Maximum for sub-task 2	<u>5</u>
Sub-task 3 – Use of Business Process Re-engineering (BPR) by A2G	
Up to 2 marks per relevant well explained point:	Up to 2 each
Definition of BPR	
Explanation of how BPR could help A2G	
Limitation of BPR for A2G	
Maximum for sub-task 3	<u>10</u>
MAXIMUM FOR TASK	<u>25</u>

Suggested solution

MEMORANDUM

To: Eleanor Tall TallE@A2G.com
Date: 14th September 20X7
Subject: Strategic considerations to be develop at A2G

Introduction

This memorandum sets out the information that you requested in relation to strategic development at A2G in relation to the use of Transaction Cost Theory, the resource-based approach versus the positioning approach and the introduction of Business Process Re-engineering.

(1) **Transaction Cost Theory**

A2G could use Transaction Cost Theory (TCT) to help it determine which activities to outsource by looking at the costs involved in such activities. The cost of in-house provision (consisting both of the specialist staff costs and the costs of the ownership of the necessary assets) would be compared with the market rate of buying that service in from a specialist supplier. This would help A2G to determine how efficient their processes are in terms of whether or not an outsourcer could provide the same service at a lower cost.

The services which should be considered for outsourcing are those which are not considered core to the business, for example payroll or cleaning would not be considered core to A2G and would therefore be suitable for outsourcing. However, A2G appears to be considering activities which could potentially be considered core to the business. TCT would be of assistance in making the decision as it will highlight which business areas the market could provide at a lower transactional cost than it currently costs in-house.

A2G must also ensure that the analysis of outsourcing versus in-house provision is considered over the long term. The company currently has state of the art assets including a sophisticated graphic design studio and TV and film production facilities along with experienced specialist staff. The costs associated with these will depend on the regularity with which they are used and the extent of asset specificity.

A2G could also consider leasing out their facilities to other advertising agencies or production companies when it is not in use as an alternative to moving to an outsource solution.

(2) **Resource-based Versus Positioning View**

A company that adopts a positioning view considers the external business environment and responds to the threats and opportunities they identify. A company that adopts a resource-based view considers their internal competences, their strengths and weaknesses, and then uses those to determine the offering they take to the external market.

If A2G is facing increased pressure from the market and a price increase is not an option, a resource-based view should be considered. This would allow A2G to focus on a particular market segment such as the entertainment industry, for example, and the company's position would hence be more secure. By focusing on one market A2G would potentially reduce the number of threats it faces from trying to serve a number of markets. As the company is partly known for the quality of its service, the market served could potentially be more secure.

Were A2G to adopt the positioning view, however, following the application of TCT, the company could be sufficiently lean to allow them to pursue whatever new opportunities come along, and do so profitably. Management would need to decide their key objectives and their general approach to the market before they realise any changes.

(3) BPR and A2G's requirements

Business process re-engineering (BPR) looks at how processes can be redesigned to improve efficiency. It can involve the introduction of significant changes to business processes - the chief tool of BPR is a clean sheet of paper.

If the issues facing A2G are due to internal inefficiencies then BPR could help in the following ways:

The BPR process starts by asking fundamental questions such as 'why we do what we do', in order to make dramatic improvements in performance. This often happens through several jobs being combined into one, increased delegation of decisions, the steps in a process being performed in a logical order.

Benchmarking exercises, comparing processes with those used in other organisations could be set up to identify more cost effective ways of doing things. Costing systems may need to be reappraised: for example it might be useful to set up activity based costing systems, to better understand the full costs involved in providing each service to the customer.

Limitations and conclusion

BPR would not benefit A2G if the causes of the declining profits are due to loss of demand or structural cost increases in the inputs such as freelance designers or studio facilities.

BPR could be of benefit to A2G through helping to realise cost savings. In the short term these changes may be expensive to implement, but the benefits should be longer-term and dramatic.

In conclusion, all three theories (transaction cost theory, resource-based view and business process re-engineering), when used in conjunction with each other could help restore A2G to profitability.

Competency coverage

Sub Task	Technical		Business acumen		People		Leadership		Integration		Max
1			•				Recommends how transaction cost theory could be used by A2G	10			10
2			Resource based vs positioning approaches for A2G	5							5
					Recommend how BPR could be used by A2G	10					10
Total				5		10		10			25

Topic 5 – E2 Further Tasks

Task 19 – ZEZ

Indicative timing: 45 minutes (excluding Background Information)

Background information

ZEZ Company is in the business of designing and printing bottle labels for soft drinks distributors. The company is, at present, facing very difficult times as recessionary economic conditions have had a negative impact on the demand for its customers' products, which in turn is having a knock-on effect on the demand for ZEZ Company's labels. As a result, the senior management team has been investigating how the company can become more efficient to ensure its future survival.

The Chief Executive has appointed the consultancy firm that you work for to provide ZEZ Company with advice during this challenging time.

Task

Today you received the following email.

From:	Chelsea Smyth cs@zez.co.uk
Sent:	12th October 20X4, 11.13am
Subject:	Conflict & negotiation

Attachments: Extract of board minutes 7th October 20X4 (Exhibit 1)

As we discussed during our meeting last week the future for ZEZ Company is looking increasingly uncertain due to tough trading conditions which currently show no signs of improvement.

In response, last week the board announced a series of redundancies across ZEZ Company. As you can see from the extract of the board minutes attached to this message (see Exhibit 1), concerns have been raised over the heightening threat of industrial action by the affected workers.

Once you have reviewed the board minutes please would you provide me with a briefing note which advises on the following matters:

- Explain the different conflict handling strategies that could be used in managing the potential conflict with the trade unions as a result of the redundancy programme.

- In light of the redundancy programme, explain the term negotiation and the different stages involved in conducting effective negotiations between senior management and the trade union representatives.

Due to the nature of the current situation I would appreciate a swift response to the points raised.

Kind regards,

Chelsea

Mrs Chelsea Smyth
Chief Executive Officer
ZEZ Company
Email: cs@zez.co.uk
Phone: 01234 456789 ext 0991

Write your response to Chelsea

Exhibit 1

ZEZ Company
Board Meeting Minutes
7th October 20X4

Chelsea Smyth - Chief Executive Officers update

'Good morning. Unfortunately I start today's meeting with bad news. As you are aware in recent times I have been closely monitoring the performance of our company as we continue to battle through extremely challenging trading conditions. Despite our ongoing best efforts, I am afraid that I have not seen the improvement needed to ensure ZEZ Company's survival without some significant measures being implemented. With this in mind I believe the time has now come for us to cut back on costs across the company in the form of an employee redundancy programme. In addition, current operating conditions mean that there will be some significant changes to the contractual terms and conditions for management and administrative staff working in various functional departments. As a result I envisage a major restructuring of our operations'.

After some discussion of the Chief Executive's suggestion the board voted in favour of the proposal, however, the following concerns were raised.

Peter McCoy - Human Resources Director

'In anticipation of a redundancy announcement, I have already been contacted by local trade union representatives acting on behalf of our employees. From my preliminary discussions it is quite clear that the trade unions will take industrial action to protect these jobs and to stop the proposed changes to the contractual terms and conditions as outlined by the Chief Executive'.

Kim Neve - Production Director

'While I fully understand why drastic action is needed to turn the company around, I am particularly concerned that a significant number of the affected staff work in the production facility. I am worried that industrial action may lead to irreparable damage to our business if production is shut down for any longer than a few days'.

TASK 20 - GN

Indicative timing: 45 minutes (excluding Background Information)

Background information

GN Holdings specialises in buying up underperforming family businesses and turning them into profitable business units. It has built up a reputation for instilling its own approach to people management, which has not always been well received by the employees working for the newly acquired companies.

You work as a management accountant for GN Holdings. In recent times the remit of your role has grown to include an increasing focus on helping operational managers improve the performance of the departments and businesses they manage.

Task

Last week you received the following email from your line manager.

From: John Stewart (johnstewart@gnholdings.co.uk)
Sent: 5th November 20X4, 8.02am
Subject: Z Company

Attachment: Article in Mergers and Acquisitions (Exhibit 1)

As you are aware we recently acquired Z Company. Unfortunately, things have not started well. Last week, respected industry journal 'Mergers and Acquisitions' ran an article highlighting the difficulties that the newly appointed management team have encountered since arriving at Z Company. The main issues raised in the article concerned the 'autocratic' leadership style being used, and the introduction of multi-skilled teams.

This is not the kind of news story that GN Holdings wants to be associated with and as a result the board of directors have asked me to come up with suggestions on how to address the issues raised by the article.

As a result I would like you to provide me with a briefing note which:

- Explains why the autocratic style of leadership adopted by the new management team is not proving effective at Z Company and provide some recommendations on how we could improve the current situation.

- Advises on the benefits of team working to help management gain the support of workers opposed to the introduction of multi-skilled teams.

I have attached a copy of the article from 'Mergers and Acquisitions' for your perusal (see Exhibit 1).

Kind regards

John

John Stewart
Head of Finance and Personnel
GN Holdings
Email: johnstewart@gnholdings.co.uk
Tel: 01234 789987 (Ext: 1239)

Write your response to John

Exhibit 1

Trouble at the top?
By Stephen Ford

Z Company is a long established family run engineering business which was recently taken over by GN Holdings. Historically relationships between managers and factory workers were very strong. Over the years this led to a contented workforce with a strong sense of loyalty towards the family owners. There was a willingness to do whatever was asked of them if it was seen to be in the best interests of the company. In the past this has been tested when at various times, workers have agreed to take a pay cut, or work longer hours when the survival of the company was threatened. In return workers have always been well cared for, enjoying excellent working conditions and a generous pension on retirement.

The last owner, Aidan Smith, was a particularly charismatic figure who many of the workers knew as a boy growing up during the time when his father was still running the business.

Unexpectedly, Aidan was recently forced to step down due to ill health. As a result the company was sold to GN Holdings. The upheaval came at a particularly difficult time for the company which had just won a major export contract that would necessitate a significant increase in output.

GN Holdings wasted no time in installing its own management team at Z Company. The new management style has not been well received and could be regarded as being autocratic. The new managers told workers that there will be changes in how their work is organised. One significant change will be the introduction of multi-skilled teams, which will mean changes to individual job roles.

Workers are unhappy and are highly sceptical about the proposed changes. Production for the export contract is now behind schedule.

TASK 21 – A Insurance Company

Indicative timing : 45 minutes (excluding Background Information)

Background information

The Direct Sales and Customer Contact Centre (the Centre) of A Insurance Company deals with vehicle, home and contents insurance products. Brenda House, who has been the manager of the Centre for the last three years, has a participative leadership style, involving staff in key decisions about the Centre. Initially she was very successful in achieving high staff morale as evidenced in the results of annual staff surveys for the first two years of her appointment. The Centre scored consistently higher on dimensions such as job satisfaction, communication and co-operation when compared with other parts of the company.

However, twelve months ago Brenda was responsible for introducing a sales target system which involved allocating staff to teams as part of a restructuring programme. Each team is set targets and the results are published on a monthly basis in a league table. The team that is top of the league receives a cash bonus.

You are a management accountant working in the finance department for A Insurance Company.

Task

Following a recent management meeting, Brenda has sent you the following email.

From: Brenda House bh@ains.co.uk
Sent: |30th June 20X4, 14.37
Subject: Sales target system

I thought you might be able to help me with some issues the Centre has been experiencing since Head Office ordered last years restructure.

A recent staff survey showed that communication and co-operation between the teams has fallen dramatically. I am worried about the growing animosity between my team leaders since the introduction of the sales target system. Recently there has been a significant increase in the levels of absenteeism, particularly in team Y. In order to improve the current situation I have been monitoring the behaviour of three teams and have noticed the following:

Team X is always at the top of the league and receives the bonus. The team leader of X is highly motivated and team spirit is high. Team members are constantly coming up with ideas on how to increase sales. The team seems to be very cohesive group and team members regularly organise social events for themselves.

Team Y never succeeds in meeting its targets. The team leader does not seem bothered by this, and appears more interested in working out how much longer he needs to work before he can retire. Team members have complained to me about the team leader, and two members have resigned. There appears to be a personality clash between the team leader and another member of the team who is viewed by the rest of the team as the 'unofficial' leader.

Team Z, whilst achieving its targets, is always behind Team X. The team members are an extremely tight knit group, but have become very insular and are no longer responsive to the work needs of other members of staff in the Centre. They appear to have their own agenda.

In light of this please could you prepare some briefing notes for me which:

- Outline the benefits and problems of introducing sales teams and sales targets in the Centre.

- Recommends appropriate strategies that could be used to minimise any problems you identify.

Kind regards

Brenda

Brenda House
Head of the Direct Sales and Customer Contact Centre
A Insurance Company
Email: bh@ains.co.uk
Phone: 01234 556771 ext 1023

Write your response to Brenda

TASK 22 - The Institute of Catering Technicians

Indicative timing: 45 minutes (excluding Background Information)

Background information

The Institute of Catering Technicians (ICT) is an organisation providing a wide range of professional and vocational awards for individuals wishing to work in the hospitality, tourism and leisure industry. Every three months (four times a year), the Institute holds examinations in 400 different examination centres all over the world. The Institute's exams are all paper based and the current system for examinations is both costly and time consuming. The board have set up a project to look at the feasibility of online marking. The Chief Executive at the Institute, Ashley Bean, has suggested that the proposed new marking process should not take longer than four weeks to complete per exam sitting.

The Institute of Catering Technicians has recently appointed the firm which you work for, Beau Consulting, to provide advice on the proposed project.

Task

You have just received the following email from Ashley Bean.

From: A.Bean@ICT.co.uk
Sent: 30th October 20X4 9:58am
Subject: Project feasibility

Thank you for agreeing to assist us during this exciting time for our Institute. I regard reducing the amount of time it takes to mark exam scripts and to issue results to candidates to be of critical importance, especially if we are to continue to attract prospective students.

To help you better understand the type of change we are proposing at ICT I have set out below our current process for marking exam scripts and the proposed new system.

Current system

1. Script answer books completed by candidates are taken from the examination room by the invigilator

2. All scripts are sent by secure courier to ICT's Head Office

3. From Head Office the scripts are sent by secure courier to individual markers

4. Once the scripts are marked they are returned to Head Office where an arithmetic check for each script is undertaken and a selection of scripts are checked for moderation to ensure that markers have correctly applied the approved marking scheme

Proposed system

1. Script answer books completed by candidates are taken from the examination room by the invigilator

2. All scripts are sent by secure courier to the Institute's local area office where scripts will be scanned onto a computer system and allocated to markers

3. The markers will gain access to the scripts via a web based software system

---

4. The script is marked by use of simple mouse movements

5. The software adds up the marks automatically which means no arithmetic script checking is required

6. The software does not allow the script to be submitted until all pages have been annotated

7. At any time the examiner can download marked scripts to undertake moderation (checking of markers' work)

As we are still at an early stage with the online marking project, I would like you to prepare briefing notes for me which:

•   Explain the different types of feasibility that should be included in the project feasibility study to assess whether or not to proceed with the project.

•   Recommend the skills that an individual would need to possess to serve as the project manager of the online marking project.

Kind regards

Ashley

Ashley Bean
Chief Executive
The Institute of Catering Technicians
Email: From: A.Bean@ICT.co.uk
Phone: 01234 456789 ext 1021

Write your response to Ashley

TASK 23 - FPC

Indicative timing: 45 minutes (excluding Background Information)

Background information

You have recently been appointed as a senior management accountant for FPC Company. The finance department has developed a very poor reputation throughout the company. The department is perceived as being poor at communicating with other functions. As a result the finance director often receives complaints from other departments. A consistent comment is that messages received from the finance department are too complicated and that too much financial jargon is used. Another common observation is that at inter-department meetings, the finance team use 'financial speak' which other members of staff find hard to understand. The finance staff are obsessed with financial indicators, and do not appreciate that there are other factors which inform decisions. It is also felt that too many emails are sent from the finance department, and it is often difficult to find the relevant information on some of the financial spreadsheets circulated which are supposed to help in decision making.

Your experience in improving the fortunes of the finance team in your previous role played a significant part in your appointment.

Task

At the end of your first week you receive the following email from the finance director.

From: Carlos Blanco (cblanco@fpc.com)
Sent: 2nd November 20X4, 12.02pm
Subject: The Finance Department

I hope your first week hasn't put you off coming back next week!

When you came in for your interview I was particularly interested to learn about the experience you gained in enhancing the status of the finance team in your old job. The reason I mention this is because I am trying to get the finance staff here at FPC to play a fuller role in the affairs of the company, becoming more integrated into the strategic and business activities of the organisation.

I know this is not going to be an easy task. Unfortunately, it appears that the finance department seems to have developed a very poor reputation in the company. I have only been working at FPC a short time myself, but during my two months with the company I have been repeatedly told by other department heads that the finance staff are generally viewed as being unhelpful.

Earlier in the week I held informal discussions with a number of staff in the department about how we could improve the working environment. Many of the staff members I spoke to felt de-motivated. I was particularly surprised to learn that none of them have been given clear individual targets and objectives. A couple of staff members mentioned that they have never received any feedback on their performance and that staff development simply has not existed. Although, there is a company-wide staff performance appraisal system in place, none of the staff in the finance department have had an appraisal in recent years.

In a bid to improve the current situation I would like you to prepare for me a briefing note which:

- Discusses the points to be covered in a series of training sessions to help members of staff in the finance department improve their communication skills.

- Advises how implementing FPC Company's appraisal system in the finance department could help improve staff performance.

Thank you for input in advance. If you have any questions please drop me an email.

Kind regards

Carlos

Carlos Blanco
Director of Finance
FPC Company
Email: cblanco@fpc.com
Telephone: 012345 678905 ext (9934)

Write your response to Carlos

TASK 24 - PRC

Indicative timing: 45 minutes (excluding Background Information)

Background information

You work as a management accountant in one of the finance departments at PRC Company. You report directly to the finance director, Lindsey Isaacs. Lindsey has worked for PRC Company for 25 years during which time she has led a number of change initiatives. She is a charismatic figure within the company and is very well respected by members of the different finance departments, with a reputation for her fairness and expert technical knowledge. Lindsey has always been a champion of the finance function, making sure that her staff enjoy excellent working conditions. As a result, the morale of the finance staff has always been high.

Task

You have just received the following email.

From: Lindsey Isaacs (lisaacs@prc.com)
Sent: 23rd February 20X5, 9.22am
Subject: Restructure

Last month at the monthly senior management meeting John Brown our new Chief Executive outlined his intentions to make a number of structural changes across the company. He repeatedly highlighted the need to improve operational effectiveness.

As you may be aware I have been asked to undertake the role of leading the re-structure of the company's finance function. The plan is that this change will involve consolidating the different finance departments across the company into a shared service centre (SSC).

I am fully aware that the move to a SSC will not be welcomed by all members of the various finance departments. Despite my announcement last week that these changes will not lead to redundancies or reductions in pay I still anticipate some resistance. A number of members of staff from the finance function have already approached me with their concerns. Two main issues keep on coming up.

Firstly, staff are concerned about working in a SSC as they believe it will lead to fewer job promotion opportunities, and secondly that they will be removed from the business units they currently serve and will end up doing more routine work which will be tightly controlled.

Please can you provide me with a briefing note which:

- Explains the benefits of PRC Company adopting a shared service centre model for the finance function.

- Recommends relevant factors that I will need to consider to ensure that staff motivation is not damaged as a result of the move to the shared service centre.

Kind regards

Lindsey

Director of Finance
PRC Company

Write your response to Lindsey

Topic 5 – E2 Further Tasks Solutions

Task 19

Marking scheme

	Marks
Sub-task 1 – Conflict handling strategies	
Up to 2 marks per relevant well explained point:	Up to 2 each
Explanation of conflict handling framework	
Avoidance	
Accommodation	
Compromise	
Competition	
Collaboration	
Maximum for sub-task 1	**13**
Sub-task 2 – Negotiation	
Up to 2 marks per relevant well explained point:	Up to 2 each
Explanation of negotiation	
Purposeful persuasion	
Constructive compromise	
Preparation	
Conducting phase	
Closing phase	
Maximum for sub-task 2	**12**
MAXIMUM FOR TASK	**25**

Suggested solution

Briefing note

To: Chelsea Smyth (ZEZ Company)
Date: 15th October 20X4
Subject: Conflict handling and stages of negotiation

Introduction

This briefing note sets out the information that you requested in relation to conflict handling strategies and the different stages of negotiation.

(1)   Conflict handling strategies

The senior management team of ZEZ Company can use a range of possible responses to handle the potential conflict. Conflict-handling strategies can be mapped on two dimensions; *assertiveness* (trying to satisfy one's own concerns) and *cooperativeness* (trying to satisfy the other party's concerns). Five of these strategies are considered below:

Avoidance. Some trivial problems blow over without particular management effort. If ZEZ Company feels that this is the case here, it can effectively deny that a problem exists and withdraw from considering it further. However, the redundancies and the threat of industrial action make this unlikely.

Accommodation. A more active policy would be to suppress the problem by smoothing over any overt disputes, in order to preserve working relationships. This approach is unlikely to produce the changes required at ZEZ Company, so the senior management team may have to combine it with a certain amount of coercion. Unless costs are reduced, ZEZ Company may not survive, and so there is little room for negotiation.

Compromise. A more positive approach for the management of ZEZ Company to take would involve a willingness to make compromises via a process of bargaining and negotiation with the trade unions. There may be some room for manoeuvre concerning the criteria for redundancy and the number of redundancies.

Collaboration. The compromise approach could be extended to a process of integration and collaboration, in which a continuing dialogue can establish both common ground and agreement as to what is required. In the case of ZEZ Company, harsh choices need to be made. Collaboration with the unions can only work if the unions accept the there will need to be changes to contractual terms and redundancies.

Competition. This is the most assertive conflict handling strategy. This is where the parties do not co-operate, but seek to maximise their own interests, and one party wins and the other loses. This approach would not be appropriate in ZEZ Company, because it would be damaging to working relationships in the long term.

(2)   **Negotiation**

Negotiation is, a process whereby two parties come together to confer with a view to concluding a jointly acceptable agreement. It is closely aligned to the 'compromise' approach outlined above.

The senior management of ZEZ Company will need to negotiate an agreement with the trade unions who are representing employees. This process is usually known as 'collective bargaining'.

The process involves two main elements:

(i)   **Purposeful persuasion**: whereby each party attempts to persuade the other to accept its case, backed by factual information and analysis. To be successful, senior management will need to persuade the unions to its viewpoint.

(ii)   **Constructive compromise**: whereby both parties accept the need to move closer toward each other's position. This involves making concessions, while still meeting the needs of both parties.

The trade union will not want to agree to job losses, but might recognise that they are inevitable and instead persuade management to provide generous severance pay and explore redeployment opportunities. Senior management, might anticipate this and work out a compromise solution.

Effective negotiation should go through a number of stages:

(i)   **Preparation**

A framework for preparing for the negotiations that ZEZ Company might use to ensure that the negotiations themselves are effective might include:

- Setting objectives for the negotiation. Deciding what ZEZ Company wants from the negotiations.

- Gathering information on the issues. For example, the proposed number of redundancies.

- Identifying potential areas of conflict.

- Identifying potential areas of movement.

- Formulating a negotiating strategy.

(ii) Conducting the negotiation

ZEZ Company may consider:

- Identifying common ground.
- Considering new proposals or counter proposals.
- Making concessions.
- Having a skilled negotiating team.
- Using effective communication skills.
- Ensuring good leadership, so that meetings can be well facilitated.

(iii) Closing the negotiation

ZEZ Company should ensure that once there is agreement, the points are written up as a draft agreement. It can then be printed, formally signed and communicated to those affected by its provisions.

I hope this briefing note has helped answer the issues raised. If you require further guidance please do not hesitate to contact me.

Competency coverage

Sub Task	Technical		Business acumen		People		Leadership		Integration		Max
1					Conflict handling strategies	13					13
2					Stages of negotiation	12					12
Total						25					25

Task 20

Marking scheme

Sub-task 1 – Current leadership style and recommendations
Up to 2 marks per relevant well explained point: Up to 2 each

Leadership style
Authoritarian/tell
Reference to theorists – applied to scenario, eg:
McGregor's Theory X
Lewin
Likert
Other

Recommendations
Participative/democratic
Reference to theorists – applied to scenario, eg:
McGregor's Theory Y
Lewin
Likert
Other
Maximum for sub-task 1   <u>13</u>

Sub-task 2 – Benefits of team working
Up to 2 marks per relevant well explained point: Up to 2 each
Development of new skills
Motivational
Fulfil social and belonging needs
Encourage greater creativity
Improve communications
Improve productivity
Other
Maximum for sub-task 2   <u>12</u>
MAXIMUM FOR TASK   <u>25</u>

Suggested solution

Briefing note

To: John Stewart (johnstewart@gnholdings.co.uk)
Date: 7th November 20X4
Subject: Z Company

Introduction

This briefing note considers the issues surrounding the leadership style currently being employed at Z Company, and the benefits that team working can bring.

(1)   Leadership style

The employees of Z Company had developed a high level of trust towards the former owners of the company. The most recent of these, Aidan Smith, was a charismatic and natural leader and as such the employees were happy to follow his direction.

GN Holdings appear to have misunderstood this willingness to follow as an autocratic approach and so this is the style that they have introduced. The approach they have adopted is consistent with McGregor's Theory X management style. This is based on the assumption that workers dislike and avoid work, are indifferent to the needs of the organisation and need constant supervision. However, the workers of Z Company have been shown to be very committed to the organisation having in the past, taken pay cuts or worked longer hours to ensure the survival of the company. The scepticism and unhappiness of the workers is therefore not surprising.

Recommendations

GN Holdings may find a democratic style more effective. This would be more in line with McGregor's Theory Y approach which assumes workers are motivated by enjoyment of their work and are prepared to work in order to meet organisational and personal goals. This may to lead to greater job satisfaction and increased levels of productivity.

This approach is supported by Lewin who also suggests that a participative or consultative leadership style is likely to bring the most benefits to the organisation and its staff. Likert's model of leadership also supports a participative or consultative style of leadership and suggests that the most effective leaders are the ones that take this approach.

These approaches are likely to work as they are based on the trust and commitment that has already been build up within Z Company.

If a participative approach was implemented at Z Company the workers would be fully involved in decision making and setting goals and schedules. A consultative approach is less extreme and would involve the managers consulting the employees and considering their opinions before any final decisions are made. Allowing employees the opportunity to voice their opinions and participate in decisions which affect them, may help the new management team to be accepted by the employees and may eventually win their trust.

(2)   Benefits of team working

The benefits of team working that the management could use to support introduction of multi-skilled teams include:

Development of new skills

Individuals could develop new skills as a result of team working. This would allow them to carry out a wider range of tasks and may have a motivating impact on workers. Developing new skills may lead to an increased ability to solve problems due to improved levels of knowledge and skills possessed by workers.

Loyalty

The collective responsibility developed may also encourage individuals to work harder in order to avoid letting the rest of the team down.

Specific responsibilities

Each team member could be given responsibilities for specific team tasks. This improves focus and avoids overload on individuals.

Fulfilment of social needs

Team membership provides regular interaction with others which can increase levels of social satisfaction and create a sense of identity, belonging and self worth. Insecurity may be reduced as team members offer support to each other.

Creativity

The input of more individuals can lead to greater levels of creativity as ideas can be bounced around between the team members.

Communication

Team working encourages better flows of information between individuals included in the team, improving the levels of communication between the workers.

Increased productivity

The organisation should also benefit from the increased productivity achieved by the team. This should arise through the effect of synergy as tasks could be broken down into component parts which could be worked on simultaneously by different team workers. Each team member would take the part which makes best use of their individual knowledge and skill set.

I hope the points raised here have been of some use. Should you wish to discuss any of the issues outlined then please do not hesitate to contact me.

Competency coverage

Sub Task	Technical		Business acumen		People		Leadership		Integration		Max
1							Leadership style and recommendations	13			13
2					Benefits of team working	12					12
Total						12		13			25

Task 21

Marking scheme

Sub-task 1 – Benefits and problems
Up to 2 marks per relevant well explained point:　　　　　　　　Up to 2 each
Identifies a range of benefits including:
Builds loyalty
Knowledge sharing
Increased participation
Builds respect
Motivational

Identifies a range of problems including:
Conflict
Isolation
Groupthink
Resentment
Maximum for sub-task 1　　　　　　　　　　　　　　　　　　　**13**

Sub-task 2 – Strategies to minimise problems
Up to 2 marks per relevant well explained point:　　　　　　　　Up to 2 each
Greater participation in target setting
Removal of cash incentives
Counselling and discipline
Mix up teams
Regular meetings
Regular briefings
Maximum for sub-task 2　　　　　　　　　　　　　　　　　　**12**
MAXIMUM FOR TASK　　　　　　　　　　　　　　　　　　　**25**

Suggested solution

Briefing note
To: Brenda House bh@ains.co.uk
Date: 2nd July 20X4
Subject: Sales teams and sales targets

Introduction

The first part of this briefing note considers the benefits and the problems of introducing the sales teams and the sales target system. The second part outlines appropriate strategies which may help to minimise the problems currently being experienced in the Centre.

(1)　**Benefits and problems of sales targets**

　　The introduction of the sales target system was aimed at increasing sales. It is not stated how the targets were set, but unless the teams were allowed to set their own targets, and measure their own progress, it is likely that the targets could be resented when not achieved.

Incentive schemes such as the one described are a common motivational technique. Given 'the Centres' success in the past it was probably never anticipated that the restructuring would have such a negative impact on working relationships, morale and productivity.

When teams rather than individuals are rewarded, it is easy for unmotivated individuals to get by with little effort. This may create resentments within the teams. However it should be noted that this does not appear to be the case in Team X at present.

As the reward in 'the Centre' is in the form of cash, it is very easy for unsuccessful teams to feel resentful and become increasingly alienated. When this happens, inter-group conflict is likely to arise.

Benefits of sales teams

Organising work groups into teams can be a powerful motivator for performance. Teams combine the skills of individuals, and fear of 'letting the side down' can be a powerful motivator. Effective teams could bring the following benefits to 'the Centre'.

(i)   Loyalty and hard work is encouraged
(ii)   Skills and information are shared
(iii)   New ideas can be tested
(iv)   Individuals are encouraged to participate
(v)   Goodwill, trust and respect can be built up
(vi)   Targets may be regularly exceeded

Team X seems to exhibit these characteristics.

Problems of sales teams

Unfortunately, Teams Y and Z are struggling in different ways. Problems identified include:

(i)   Conflict and personality problems can arise, as has happened in Team Y. Informal networks come to the fore, which may work against overall organisational objectives.

(ii)   The rigid nature of the new team-based structure has meant that Team Z has abandoned the rest of 'the Centre'.

(iii)   Group consensus (groupthink) can stifle thought and isolate the team. This appears to have happened to Team Z.

(2)   **Strategies to minimise problems**

Working on the assumption that the team structure cannot be disbanded you could consider the following strategies to address the current problems:

Participation in target setting

This may help the team members to 'buy-in' to the targets, and encourage them to see these as achievable.

Split teams by product

It may be possible to give each team its own product (eg vehicle, home, and contents insurance) rather than having them compete directly, reward them on percentage improvement each month or quarter. As all products may be bought by one customer this may encourage cross-team co-operation, in such cases it may be more appropriate to reward all teams when overall sales are increased.

Incentives

Removing the cash incentive, and replacing it with a reward that is less emotive and less likely to cause resentment may improve the situation, eg a 'team of the month' trophy or similar prize. A 'suggestion box', independent of team membership, should be set up to reward individual ideas.

Mix up the teams

This may help to shake up the cliques and insularity that have formed and preventing proper co-operation. Reference to Belbin's roles should ensure that teams have a good mix of people.

Regular meetings of all team members

These may encourage cooperation between teams, reinforce organisational objectives and provide a mechanism for conflicts to be resolved. Informal networks may be formed, with social events involving all teams encouraged.

Counselling and discipline

The leader of Team Y is not performing and this is adversely affecting the team. This needs to be sorted out by way of counselling or some sort of disciplinary procedure.

Team leader briefings

Regular team leader briefings should be held, so that team leaders can keep their members up to date with organisational developments. This may reduce the potential for animosity between the teams and help reduce the incidence of groupthink in Team Z.

I hope the points raised here have been of some use. Should you wish to discuss any of the issues outlined then please do not hesitate to contact me.

Competency coverage

Sub Task	Technical		Business acumen		People		Leadership		Integration		Max
1					Benefits and problems of introducing sales teams and sales targets	13					13
2							Strategies to minimise problems	12			12
Total						13		12			25

Task 22

Marking scheme

	Marks
Sub-task 1 – Types of feasibility	
Up to 2 marks per relevant well explained point:	Up to 2 each
Purpose	
Technical feasibility explanation and application	
Social feasibility explanation and application	
Ecological feasibility explanation and application	
Financial feasibility explanation and application	
Maximum for sub-task 1	**13**
Sub-task 2 - Project manager skills	
Up to 2 marks per relevant well explained point:	Up to 2 each
Leadership explanation and application	
Communication explanation and application	
Negotiation explanation and application	
Delegation explanation and application	
Change management explanation and application	
Maximum for sub-task 2	**12**
MAXIMUM FOR TASK	**25**

Suggested solution

Briefing note

To: A.Bean@ICT.co.uk
Date: 3rd November 20X4
Subject: Project feasibility and project management skills

Introduction

This briefing note considers the different types of feasibility that should be considered when assessing the online marking project and provides recommendations on the skills needed to serve as the project manager.

(1) **Purpose**

The purpose of the feasibility study is to provide information during the decision-making process over whether or not the online marking project should proceed. It will determine whether the projects objectives can be met in a cost effective manner and determine the best strategy to achieve the project.

The types of feasibility to be considered may include:

Technical feasibility

The project is technically feasible if the required technology exists, has been tested and is available for use. It would appear that this is the case.

The technology (including marking software, scanners and any other related infrastructure) will need to be reviewed to ensure that performance levels meet the needs of the ICT.

The scanners themselves and the processes relating to exam script scanning will have to be considered to ensure the technical feasibility of scanning scripts to the required quality within tight deadlines can be met. Controls relating to the number of scripts scanned and ensuring all pages of each script have been scanned will also have to be reviewed.

The ICT will need to determine whether it will provide computers or require the markers to use their own, in which case they may need to issue minimum system requirement guidelines. The data security of the software will have to be reviewed along with the ability of the supplier to ensure scripts can be accessed at all times during the marking period.

Social (operational) feasibility

The project will be operationally feasible if it is aligned with the organisation's goals and environment. Key considerations for the ICT may include providing training to markers, and the possibility of redundancies needed at head office to reflect the reduction of physical processes.

Ecological (environmental) feasibility

Ecological feasibility considers the impact of the project in terms of pollution, the effect on the local community, and the impact on the reputation of the ICT. The project will reduce transport pollution when moving scripts during the marking process, and so has a positive environmental effect.

Financial (economic) viability

The financial viability of a project can be assessed using a cost benefit analysis. Costs may include capital items such as the hardware (scanners) and software; revenue costs may include training and maintenance, and finance costs may include any interest payable on loans taken out to finance the project.

Tangible benefits may include the reduction in courier costs and head office staff costs (however, the associated redundancy costs will also have to be considered); intangible benefits may include a faster and more efficient marking process leading to a quicker release of results to students and an improved image of the ICT.

(2) **Leadership skills**

The project manager will need strong leadership skills in order to obtain cooperation, good performance, and results from the project team members. The manager will need an understanding of different management styles so that an appropriate approach can be taken at each stage of the project.

Communication skills

In order to ensure the project progresses, the project manager must be able to regularly and effectively communicate with a number of people including the project team, suppliers of the software and the markers. Progress reports will also have to be provided to the project sponsor.

Negotiation skills

The project manager will need negotiation skills. Negotiation may be required to determine the timescales and schedules of work between the project team and the software supplier. Good negotiation skills may be needed to help prevent any conflicts which arise during the project.

Delegation skills

Project tasks will need to be delegated to appropriate staff. The project manager should provide responsibility and a sense of ownership to the team members to encourage collaboration and team work. The project manager should then monitor the output of the team and be prepared to intervene should problems arise.

Change management skills

The online marking project represents a fundamental shift in the ICT's approach. It is therefore crucial that the project manager has the necessary change management skills to ensure the project is a success.

I hope these notes have been of some use, please do not hesitate to contact me should you wish to discuss any of the points raised.

Competency coverage

Sub Task	Technical		Business acumen		People		Leadership		Integration		Max
1			Types of feasibility	13							13
2							Recommends the required skills to be project manager	12			12
Total				13						12	25

Task 23

Marking scheme

Marks

Sub-task 1 – Training sessions

Up to 2 marks per relevant well explained point: Up to 2 each
Communication model and its elements
Need for the sender to understand purpose of communications
Need for sender to understand level of knowledge and interests of recipients
Problems with use of technical language and jargon
Problems with the form of messages and channels of communication: e-mails and spreadsheets
Value of combining non-financial with financial performance indicators
Value of feedback and monitoring use of information
Communications planning

Maximum for sub-task 1   <u>13</u>

Sub-task 2 - Appraisal system

Up to 2 marks per relevant well explained point: Up to 2 each
Defining performance standards and giving direction to individuals. Reference to finance department
Monitoring performance of individuals against targets
Appraisal schemes and incentive/reward schemes
Identifying good performance and weaknesses in performance
Development of the individual; using appraisal schemes to plan training and development measures
Motivation of individuals
Maximum for sub-task 2   12
MAXIMUM FOR TASK   <u>25</u>

Suggested solution

To: Carlos Blanco
Date: 6th November 20X4
Subject: Communication and appraisals

This briefing note sets out the key points which should be included in the proposed training sessions and advises how FPC's appraisal system could help improve staff performance in the finance department.

(1)   **Communications model**

Training should initially focus on the communication problems that exist in the department. As a way of structuring the problems these could be presented using a simple communication model. A basic communication model consists of the creator and consumers, the message, the language of the message and the medium for transmitting the message. Training should encourage finance staff to understand that problems in communication can occur with any of these, making the communication process ineffective.

The creator

Staff need to recognise the level of understanding of the recipients of information. In the case of financial information, it is particularly important to recognise that non-financial staff do not have a strong understanding of the technicalities of finance and are unlikely to understand the jargon that finance staff commonly use. Awareness needs to be established that finance department messages are often too complicated. Training should include methods of presenting relatively simple messages in language that the recipients can understand.

The recipient

Communications should mean something to the recipient and should prompt the recipient into action where appropriate. This means that the messages should 'grab their attention' and sustain their interest. Messages should therefore highlight information that matters. Finance staff need to understand that recipients of information respond to messages about non-financial as well as financial matters, and may be disinclined to study financial indicators alone.

The medium

Staff need to be trained to recognise the importance of using suitable communication channels for messages. We are told that there is excessive use of e-mails and financial spreadsheets in which it is difficult to identify relevant information. It might help to make finance staff aware of the number of e-mails that managers in FPC have to deal with each day, and how they respond to the many e-mails they receive.

Training could focus on whether other methods of presenting information – for example in graphical form might be more appropriate.

Feedback

Training sessions should get finance staff to understand the value of feedback, and the need to monitor how recipients have responded to the messages sent out. If information is not being used in the manner intended, measures need to be taken to make the messages more effective.

To bring the training to an end it may be useful to establish a communications plan for use in the finance department which covers the purpose of information, its content, form, timing, avoiding the use of technical language or jargon, and monitoring how it is understood and used.

(2) **Staff appraisal**

In the finance department staff do not have clear targets or objectives. When there are annual appraisals for members of staff, the process can be used to establish performance standards and targets. Informing individuals about what is expected of them might encourage them to work in conformity or towards stated goals.

Annual appraisals can then be used to monitor actual performance by comparing it against the target, meaning that individuals can be made aware of how well or how badly they have performed. Praising good performance may motivate individuals to maintain their standards in the future.

Appraisal schemes are often linked to reward schemes, and annual bonuses for achieving or exceeding targets. A criticism of reward schemes is that individuals may focus on achieving targets to the exclusion of all other considerations. This highlights the need for incentive schemes to be carefully structured.

Appraisal schemes can encourage the personal development of individual employees. Appraisal interviews can be used to discuss with individual team members what they have achieved in the year, and what they have done well or badly. This constructive discussion can be used to consider ways of improving performance and helping the individuals future development eg through training or greater role responsibility. This may have a motivating effect.

Appraisal interviews should happen regularly, typically once a year. If they are held infrequently, as in the finance department, they will be ignored as nothing more than an occasional wasteful administrative exercise by the HR department. There should however be continual monitoring and mentoring of individuals throughout the year, to improve and sustain their personal development.

I hope these notes have been of some use, please do not hesitate to contact me should you wish to discuss any of the points raised.

Competency coverage

Sub Task	Technical		Business acumen		People		Leadership		Integration		Max
1					Points for consideration in the training sessions	13					13
2					Appraisal system and improving staff performance	12					12
Total						25					25

Task 24

Marking scheme

Marks

Sub-task 1 – Benefits of PRC Company adopting a SSC

Up to 2 marks per relevant well explained point: — Up to 2 each
Defines SSC
Overhead cost reduction
Improved consistency
Knowledge sharing
Improved quality of service to other departments
Maximum for sub-task 1 — <u>8</u>

Sub-task 2 – Factors to avoid damaging staff motivation

Up to 2 marks per relevant well explained point: — Up to 2 each
Herzberg's theory of motivation
Motivating factors explained and applied
Hygiene factors explained and applied
Job enlargement and job enrichment
Leadership style
Career development
Recognition scheme
Maximum for sub-task 2 — <u>17</u>

MAXIMUM FOR TASK — <u>25</u>

Suggested solution

Briefing note

To: Lindsey Isaacs (lisaacs@prc.com)
Date: 24th February 20X5
Subject: Restructure queries

Introduction

This briefing note outlines the benefits of PRC Company adopting a shared service centre model and those factors that you will need to consider in order to avoiding damaging staff motivation.

(1) Benefits to PRC Company

Shared service centres (SSC) consolidate the transaction-processing activities within a company. SSC's aim to achieve significant cost reductions while improving service levels through the use of standardised technology and processes. At PRC Company this will involve combining the various finance departments within the organisation to form a single function.

PRC Company will experience a significant reduction in overhead costs as a result of this move. Adopting the SSC approach should lead to improved consistency in the management of finance data across PRC Company, as opposed to every finance department pursuing their own methods.

This should lead to improved quality of service for the departments dependent on the finance function. Arguably, the sharing of knowledge is enhanced when finance teams are located together in one location.

(2) Factors for consideration

To ensure staff morale and motivation are not damaged as a result of the move to a SSC, consideration should be given to Hertzberg's theory of motivation. Herzberg identified that so called hygiene factors need to be in place to reduce staff dissatisfaction. If they are absent this can lead to dissatisfaction and consequently impact on performance. Hygiene factors may include for example, pay, the working environment and company policy. These factors tend to be extrinsic to the job itself.

By contrast, Herzberg's motivating factors are those which if present can motivate individuals to superior effort and performance. Motivating factors may include challenging work or workplace recognition. They tend to be related to the job itself, in other words are intrinsic factors and are referred to as motivators or growth factors.

Applying this theory to the SSC it seems likely that the hygiene factors such as competitive salaries and good working conditions will already be in place. However, there are some hygiene factors that need attention, specifically the concern about the nature of supervision. It will be important that the work design in the SSC does not come across as close supervision which would be problematic to professional finance staff used to making their own decisions.

Consideration should also be given to potential motivating factors, such as those relating to recognition, challenging work, responsibility and advancement. Particular attention should be given to the design of jobs within the SSC, and the possibilities for job enlargement and job enrichment. This would involve exploring the design of job roles in the SSC to ensure interesting and challenging work is provided to staff.

It will be important that the style of leadership in the SSC is participative, rather than autocratic and that the finance staff are given responsibility for their own area of work and encouraged to participate in decision making, with managers providing constructive feedback on individual performance.

A further recommendation would be to look at how prospects for career development could be achieved in the SSC. This might mean providing opportunities for lateral moves to enable staff to gain new experiences and competencies.

Consideration should be given to the introduction of some kind of recognition scheme in the SSC especially as recognition is an important motivator. This could be achieved, at one level, by simply encouraging managers to thank members of staff for their contribution, acknowledging extra effort and performance as the SSC is established. More formal recognition systems could also be considered which provide staff with financial rewards in recognition of good performance.

I hope these notes have been of some use, please do not hesitate to contact me should you wish to discuss any of the points raised.

Competency coverage

Sub Task	Technical		Business acumen		People		Leadership		Integration		Max
1			Benefits of SSC for PRC's finance function	8							8
2							Recommendation of relevant factors	17			17
Total				8					17		25

Topic 6 – F2 Task Practice

The Practice Tasks that follow are intended to serve several purposes:

- They are spread across the key topics in the syllabus, to enable you to recap important areas of technical knowledge

- Although not based on the real preseen they have been designed to reflect the style of the Tasks in the ICS Exam, so that you can use them to develop your ICS Exam Technique

- Note that as they are not based on a separate preseen, they contain more background/scenario information than you would expect in the 'unseen' Tasks in your real exam.

- The solutions are intended to be "student achievable" and reflective of the level of detail CIMA provide in their Examiners Solutions.

- They should provide you with a good range of business situations that could be applied to the real preseen. As well as attempting each Practice Task in its own right, you should also take some to reflect afterwards as to how the issues you've worked through could relate to the real preseen organisation.

Topic 6 – F2 Primary Tasks

Task 25 - Newnham

Indicative timing: 45 minutes (excluding Background Information)

Background information

Newnham, a public limited company, builds, develops and operates airports. The majority of the shares are owned by large institutional investors. The finance director, Jeremy Hill, has recently retired and his replacement, Kate Smith is looking for guidance on the accounting treatment for several complex transactions.

You are the Financial Controller and have been for a number of years. The financial statements of Newnham for the year ended 31 December 20X0 are currently being prepared.

On 1 October 20X0, the following article was published in a national newspaper:

Newnham lands in trouble

At 10am today, a section of the busy city airport of Stowhampton collapsed and as a result, several passengers were rushed to the local hospital with serious injuries. The terminal has now been closed until further notice.

It is widely believed that the accident is the fault of the airport operator, Newnham. It is therefore expected that relatives of the injured passengers will take legal action against Newnham.

This afternoon, the chief executive officer, Tom Hough, announced that an immediate investigation would be launched to identify the reason for the collapse.

Task

As the accounts department are finalising the financial statements of Newnham for the year ended 31 December 20X0, you receive this email:

From:	Kate Smith ks@newnham.co.uk
Sent:	10th February 20X1, 10.15 a.m.
Subject:	Financial statements for year ended 31 December 20X0

My accounting knowledge is a little rusty and I need your help on the accounting treatment for two items (see Exhibit 1).

In relation to the airport collapse in October, I do not think that the conditions for recognising a provision or disclosing a contingent liability in respect of legal compensation and damages have been met and therefore, no accounting entries or disclosures are required in the financial statements for the year ended 31 December 20X0.

Regarding our shareholding in Bodair, I do not believe we should account for the investment as an associate because we hold less than 20% of the voting rights and do not have significant influence. I feel that the majority owner of Bodair uses its influence as the parent to control and govern its subsidiary. On this basis, I believe that in Newnham's individual and group financial statements, we should treat the investment in Bodair as a simple available for sale financial asset. I don't think there is any need to disclose the sale of the software licence nor the provision of business advice.

Please could you prepare a report explaining whether the above proposed accounting treatment complies with International Financial Reporting Standards (IFRSs) for each of:

• the airport collapse; and

• the investment in Bodair;

If you propose an alternative accounting treatment, please explain your reasons.

Kind regards,

Kate

Kate Smith

Finance Director

Newnham

E: ks@newnham.co.uk

T: 0208 345 1234

Write the report requested by Kate Smith.

Exhibit 1

Information provided by the finance director, Kate Smith, to assist in the preparation of financial statements for the year ended 31 December 20X0

Airport collapse

The investigation into the accident and the reconstruction of the section of the airport damaged are still in progress. No legal action has yet been brought in connection with the accident. The expert report that was to be presented to the civil courts in order to determine the cause of the accident and to assess the responsibility of the various parties involved is expected in early 20X1.

Financial damages arising relate to the additional costs and operating losses arising from the unavailability of the building. The nature and extent of the damages, and the details of any compensation payments have yet to be established.

Interest in Bodair

Newnham is one of three shareholders in a regional airport, Bodair. As at 31 December 20X0, the majority shareholder held 60.1% of the voting shares, the second shareholder held 20% of the voting shares and Newnham held 19.9% of the voting shares. The board of directors consisted of ten members. The majority shareholder was represented by six of the board members, while Newnham and the other shareholder were represented by two members each. A shareholders' agreement stated that certain board and shareholder resolutions require unanimous or majority decision. There is no indication that the majority shareholder and the other shareholders act together in a common way.

During the year, Newnham sold Bodair a software licence for $5 million and sent a team of management experts to give business advice to the board of Bodair.

END OF TASK

Task 26 – MT

Indicative timing: 45 minutes (excluding Background Information)

Background information

You are the Chief Financial Officer of MT, a public limited company operating in the food industry. The majority of MT Group's sales relate to organic produce with the exception of two of its subsidiaries, AB and CD. AB specialises in pre-mixed alcoholic cocktails, selling to supermarkets, bars and hotels. CD's key product is frozen ready meals with budget supermarkets being the key customer.

The finance department are currently in the process of finalising the financial statements for the year ended 30 June 20X5:

Statements of profit or loss for the year ended 30 June 20X5

	MT Group (excluding AB and CD) $'m	AB $'m	CD $'m
Revenue	2,000	1,500	800
Cost of sales	(1,200)	(1,000)	(500)
Gross profit	800	500	300
Distribution costs	(400)	(120)	(80)
Administrative expenses	(240)	(250)	(100)
Other income	40	–	–
Profit before tax	200	130	120
Income tax expense	(50)	(40)	(20)
Profit for the year	150	90	100
Gross margin	40.0%	33%	37.5%
Net margin	7.5%	6%	12.5%

Sam Waddon, the Chief Executive Officer, is worried about recent adverse publicity regarding the activities of its subsidiaries:

Extract from a national newspaper on 10 August 20X5

Overweight MT needs to kick the booze and junk food

With approximately 2.5 million alcohol-related deaths worldwide annually, it is time for the corporate giants, such as MT, to take responsibility. MT prides itself on sales of healthy organic products. However, one of its subsidiaries manufactures fruit-flavoured alcoholic cocktails whilst another sells frozen ready meals.

How can MT stand by its slogan 'greener, happier, healthier' when some of its products are contributing to the worldwide obesity epidemic?

Task

On 16 August 20X5, you receive the following email from the Chief Executive Officer, Sam Waddon:

From:	Sam Waddon sw@mt.co.uk
Sent:	16 August 20X5 9.30 a.m.
Subject:	Preparation for board meeting on 20 August 20X5

Yesterday I circulated a proposal for the sale of shares in AB and CD (see Exhibit 1). I would like you to prepare me a briefing paper in advance of the board meeting on 20 August 20X5. You can assume that these disposals will take place in the year ended 30 June 20X6.

I am concerned about the recent adverse impact on our share price of the negative publicity arising from the newspaper article of 10 August and would like to understand what potential impact my strategic plan will have on earnings and share price.

Please could you prepare a report which:

- Explains how the planned disposals should be accounted for in the consolidated financial statements of the MT Group for the year ended 30 June 20X6; and

- Briefly outlines the potential impact of the planned disposals on group earnings (using 20X5 figures as 20X6 figures are unknown) and the share price.

No calculations are required at this stage.

Write the report requested by Sam Waddon in the email above.

Exhibit 1

Proposal by Sam Waddon to board members on 15 August 20X5 (circulated in advance of the board meeting on 20 August 20X5)

In light of the fact that our subsidiaries, AB and CD, are no longer a strategic fit, I am looking to divest our shareholdings in these entities.

Fruit-based alcoholic beverages are particularly damaging to our core brand due to adverse publicity around increasing rates of alcohol-related diseases and their particular appeal to the teenage market. Therefore, I would like to dispose of our full 90% shareholding in AB.

However, with CD, due to its stronger net margin, I would like to gradually divest of our shareholding, retaining a controlling interest for the forthcoming year. My plan is to reduce our 75% shareholding to a 65% shareholding in the year ended 30 June 20X6.

END OF TASK

Task 27 – PaperGlo

Indicative timing: 60 minutes (excluding Background Information)

Background information

PaperGlo is an unlisted Australian stationery retailer. The company prides itself of having a low environmental footprint by selling mainly online with only three retail outlets in Sydney, Perth and Melbourne. Its products are manufactured from sustainable, recycled raw materials and are purchased from an approved suppliers list. Electricity for its head office is generated from solar panels. PaperGlo has won many international environmental best practice awards. PaperGlo prepares its financial statements in accordance with International Financial Reporting Standards (IFRS).

Pete Watts is the chief executive officer of PaperGlo which he began as a small family-run business twenty years ago. Since then, the company has grown rapidly, gradually increasing its market share to become the largest stationery retailer in Australia. However, Pete's family members still retain a controlling shareholding.

Pete Watts is now looking to expand the business and feels that the first step should be to acquire one of its suppliers to move the manufacturing in-house with the aim of improving gross margins. He has identified a New Zealand company, Biggle, an environmentally-friendly manufacturer of stationery supplies, as a potential target. If the acquisition were to go ahead, PaperGlo would stop using its other suppliers (which are all based in Australia) and use Biggle for all of their manufacturing. As PaperGlo's sales are all currently to domestic customers, by acquiring a manufacturer in New Zealand, Pete hopes to be able to break into the New Zealand stationery retail market. Biggle also prepares its financial statements in accordance with IFRS and reports in the New Zealand dollar (NZ$).

You are Naomi Griffiths, the financial controller of PaperGlo and you report to the finance director, Guy Jackman.

Extracts from Biggle's latest annual report are shown below.

Financial statements for Biggle for the year ended 30 September 20X4

The statement of financial position as at 30 September 20X4 and its comparative is shown below:

	20X4 NZ$m	20X3 NZ$m
ASSETS		
Non-current assets		
Property, plant and equipment	480	404
Investment in associate	177	–
Available for sale investments	150	140
	807	544
Current assets		
Inventories	145	65
Receivables	247	134
Cash and cash equivalents	–	22
	392	221
Total assets	1,199	765
EQUITY AND LIABILITIES		
Equity		
Share capital	100	100
Revaluation reserve	74	32
Other reserves	32	22
Retained earnings	457	333
Total equity	663	487
Non-current liabilities		
Loans	400	210
Current liabilities		
Payables	99	68
Overdraft	37	–
	136	68
Total liabilities	536	278
Total equity and liabilities	1,199	765

The statement of profit or loss and other comprehensive income for the year ended 31 December 20X4 and its comparative is shown below:

	20X4 NZ$m	20X3 NZ$m
Revenue	1,430	1,022
Cost of sales	(1,058)	(705)
Gross profit	372	317
Administrative expenses	(74)	(62)
Distribution costs	(158)	(100)
Finance costs	(60)	(30)
Share of profit of associate	80	–
Profit before tax	160	125
Income tax expense	(40)	(33)
Profit for the year	120	92
Other comprehensive income:		
Revaluation gain on property, plant and equipment	45	15
Gains on available for sale investments	16	6
Tax effects of other comprehensive income	(14)	(5)
Other comprehensive income for the year, net of tax	47	16
Total comprehensive income for the year	167	108

Biggle: Extract from the Chairman's statement for the year ended 30 September 20X4

Throughout the year ended 30 September 20X4, we have been implementing an expansion strategy aimed at pursuing new markets within our existing product base. Our products are now being sold in supermarkets as well as specialised stationery stores.

In January 20X4, Biggle won a new contract to supply a European supermarket chain so for the first time, as well as continuing to sell to our domestic market, we now have an overseas presence.

I am delighted to report that this expansion has resulted in 40% increase in revenue and a $28 million increase in the profit for the year.

To increase our market share, we acquired a highly profitable associate in February 20X4 and invested in non-current assets during the year. These non-current assets include machines designed with cutting-edge technology designed to minimise harmful emissions. We are pleased to announce that our strategy of maximising sustainability through use of recycled materials and generating power in our factories from renewable energy has resulted in Biggle winning the New Zealand Award for Environmental Excellence for the fifth year in a row.

20X4 is a year to be proud of!

Task

On 10 April 20X5, you receive the following email from Guy Jackman:

From:	Guy Jackman gj@paperglo.au
Sent:	10 April 20X5 9.30 am
Subject:	Potential acquisition of Biggle

Naomi,

As you are probably aware, Pete is looking to improve gross margins through the acquisition of a supplier. He has identified a New Zealand company, Biggle as a potential target. He has asked us to prepare an initial analysis of Biggle which he can use for the board meeting on 15 April. I have calculated some useful ratios (Exhibit 1) to assist with this analysis so there is no need for any further calculations at this stage.

Pete would like to raise equity finance to fund the acquisition and is thinking about seeking a listing for PaperGlo on the Australian Securities Exchange to gain access to a wider pool of investors. He has asked me whether there are any potential disadvantages to PaperGlo of seeking this listing. I think that you are in a good position to help me with this given that you were employed by a listed company for the duration of your training contract.

Please could you prepare some briefing notes in the form of an email to assist Pete in his preparation for the forthcoming board meeting that:

- Analyse the financial performance of Biggles;

- Analyse the financial position of Biggles; and

- Explain the potential disadvantages to PaperGlo of seeking a listing.

In your analysis, although the main focus should be financial, please also briefly consider non-financial aspects and make sure you conclude with a preliminary recommendation as to whether the investment in Biggle should be considered further.

Many thanks.

Best wishes,

Guy

Prepare the briefing notes requested by Guy Jackman.

Exhibit 1

Biggle: Key ratios

	20X4	20X3
Gross profit margin	26%	31%
Operating profit margin (excluding associate)	9.8%	15.2%
Non-current asset turnover	3.0 times	2.5 times
Gearing (debt/equity) (including overdraft as debt)	66%	43%
Quick ratio	1.8	2.3
Inventory days	50 days	34 days
Receivables days	63 days	48 days
Payable days	34 days	35 days

END OF TASK

Task 28 – T Company

Indicative timing: 45 minutes (excluding Background Information)

Background information

T Company has for many years operated as a family owned business producing gift boxes, wrapping paper and greetings cards. The company is one in which everyone knows everyone else and all employees participate in some way in the day to day running of the business. The owner/manager, Z, is always open to new ideas from any member of staff since he feels that local knowledge is important to decision making. He encourages staff to be flexible in their roles within the company, depending on business needs.

New staff tends to be recruited locally and often follow others from their family into the company. Many of the current management positions are held by employees with no formal management training or qualifications, but who have worked their way up from junior positions within T Company. Z prides himself on knowing the names of all his staff and takes time to ask them about their families and interests. He also tries to attend the many social events the employees arrange and plays for the company's football team.

T Company operates in T-Land where the currency is the T$.

You are a member of the senior management team of T Company. Z has made a recent announcement to employees (see below).

Announcement by Z to employees on 30 September 20X5

> 'It is with some regret that I have to make this announcement today. T Company is going to be sold to a much larger international organisation, SW Group. Whilst I anticipate that most employees should be able to keep their job, the acquiring organisation will have its own way of doing business. In the future, you will have to accept a much more bureaucratic approach which would be quite different to how things have operated in the past. The new senior management team would be appointed from within SW Group's other companies.'

Task

Shortly after the announcement of the sale of T Company to SW Group, you receive the following email:

From:	z@tcompany.co.uk
Sent:	2nd October 20X5, 9.10 a.m.
Subject:	Sale of T Company to SW Group

As a trusted member of the senior management team of T Company, I need your help. I am worried about the impact of the sale of T Company to SW Group on the morale of employees. I would like employees to better understand the impact of the potential change in management style following the acquisition.

Furthermore, as SW Group is primarily located overseas in A-land and the currency of the group accounts will be the A$, I need the accounting team to understand how to translate the financial statements of T Company for inclusion in the consolidated financial statements of SW Group. I have drafted some information to assist with this (Exhibit 1).

Please could you prepare me a briefing note that:

- Compares and contrasts the way in which T Company is currently managed and how it is likely to be managed in the future, following its acquisition by SW Group; and

- Explains what the functional currency of T Company will adopt following the acquisition by the SW Group and how the financial statements of T Company will be translated for inclusion in the consolidated financial statements of SW Group.

I can then use your briefing note in the form of an email as a basis for my discussion with employees.

Kind regards,

Z

Manager

T Company

E: z@tcompany.co.uk

T: 01449 644573

Write the briefing note requested by Z in the email above.

Exhibit 1

Information to assist in incorporating T Company into SW Group's consolidated financial statements

(a)	SW Group prepare their consolidated financial statements in A$ as they primarily operate in A-Land.
(b)	After the acquisition, with the exception of the new management team being appointed from SW Group, T Company will continue to operate independently.
(c)	T Company will continue to make the majority of sales in T-Land in the T$. Existing employees will largely be retained and will be continued to be paid in T$. Goods will continue to be purchased locally.
(d)	The level of intragroup transactions between T Company and SW Group is anticipated to be low. It is expected that T Company will generate sufficient cash flows to be able to service its own borrowings.

END OF TASK

Task 29 – MiniMark

Indicative timing: 45 minutes (excluding Background Information)

Background information

MiniMark Co is a large listed supermarket chain. The Finance Director of MiniMark Co, Claire James, has recently reorganised the finance department following several years of growth within the business, which now includes a number of overseas operations.

The company now has separate treasury and financial control departments.

The Chief Executive Officer (CEO), Douglas Wallis, has been in the post for the last five years and is one of the highest paid CEO's in the industry.

You are Alex Hill, the Financial Controller reporting directly to Claire James.

A newspaper article about MiniMark Co has recently appeared in the national press. An extract has been included below.

Extract from a national newspaper on 10th January 20X7

Fat cat votes to get fatter!

MiniMark Co, the international supermarket chain has taken fat cat salaries to a new level. Despite failing to increase profit for the last 5 years and announcing a pay freeze for employees, the Chief Executive Officer Douglas Wallis has just awarded himself and his fellow directors an inflation-busting 10% pay rise and a cash bonus equivalent to 50% of their already bloated salaries.

Outspoken boss Wallis earned $2 million in salary before bonus last year, more than 100 times the wages of the average shelf-stacker.

Task

A few days after the newspaper article, you receive an email from Claire James:

From:	Claire Jamescj@minimark.co.uk
Sent:	16th January, 2.15 p.m.
Subject:	Share-based payments; treasury and financial control departments

Following the board meeting last week, Douglas Wallis has asked me to draft a memorandum. I am so busy at the moment with year end that I could really do with your help. Before you start, please read through last week's board minutes (Exhibit 1). You will see that Douglas is considering replacing the directors' cash-based bonus with a share-based payment. He is also struggling to understand the roles of the finance and treasury control departments and the relevance of a balance scorecard approach in the context of MiniMark Co.

Please could you draft a memorandum which:

- Explains how the directors' bonus would be accounted for if it were a share-based payment and which type of share-based payment might be preferred by the market;

- Distinguishes the financial control function from the treasury function, identifying any areas of interaction between the two functions; and

- Explain the ways in which the balanced scorecard approach could be used to appraise the financial control function.

I know that you have recently completed an evening class on management techniques so I think you are excellently placed to explain how the balanced scorecard approach could be applied to the finance function of MiniMark Co.

Kind regards,

Claire James

Finance Director

MiniMark Co

E: cj@mimimark.co.uk

T: 01225 123 556

Write the memorandum requested by Claire James in the email above.

Exhibit 1

Extract from board minutes on 15ᵗʰ January 20X7

Douglas Wallis mentioned that he was worried about the impact on MiniMark Co's share price of the bad publicity resulting from the directors' pay rise and bonus. Claire James suggested that replacing the cash bonus with a share-based payment would align the directors' and shareholders' interests and would probably go down better with the market. Douglas Wallis said he thought a share-based payment would be a good idea as no expense would need to be recorded since no cash would be involved.

Douglas Wallis also mentioned that he was not entirely clear on the exact responsibilities of the new treasury and financial control departments, and whilst he liked the idea in principle, he would like a better understanding of their roles. Claire James mentioned that she would ask the Financial Controller to brief him on the differences. Claire then went on to explain that she was considering the use of the balanced scorecard approach in appraising the effectiveness of the finance function. Douglas Wallis asked Claire to brief him on how this could be done.

END OF TASK

Task 30 – PZ Group

Indicative timing: 45 minutes (excluding Background Information)

Background information

The PZ Group comprises two companies: P Limited and Z Limited. Both companies manufacture similar items and are located in different regions of the same country. Return on capital employed (ROCE) is used as the group's performance measure and is also used to determine divisional managers' bonuses. The group's financing and transfer pricing policy is determined centrally by the Board, without input from the division managers.

You are the financial controller of the PZ Group and you report directly to the Finance Director, Richard Smith. The Chief Executive Officer of the PZ Group, Graham Tagg, has been recently appointed and was previously the chief executive officer of a key competitor of the PZ Group.

Extracts from the financial statements of P Limited, Z Limited and the PZ Group have been included below.

Extracts from the financial statements of the two companies and of the group for the year ended 31 December 20X0

	P Limited $'000	Z Limited $'000	PZ Group $'000
Revenue	200,000	220,000	400,000
Cost of sales	(170,000)	(160,000)	(310,000)
Gross profit	30,000	60,000	90,000
Administrative expenses	(10,000)	(30,000)	(40,000)
Finance costs	(10,000)		(10,000)
Profit before tax	10,000	30,000	40,000
Non-current assets:			
Original cost	1,000,000	1,500,000	2,500,000
Accumulated depreciation	(590,400)	(1,106,784)	(1,697,184)
Carrying amount	409,600	393,216	802,816
Net current assets	50,000	60,000	110,000
	459,600	453,216	912,816
Non-current borrowings	150,000		150,000
Equity	309,600	453,216	762,816
Capital employed	459,600	453,216	912,816

Notes	
1.	During the year Z Limited sold goods to P Limited that had cost Z Limited $10 million for $20 million, which P Limited paid for in cash. All of the goods have been sold to external customers by the year end. The transactions relating to this sale have been eliminated from the PZ Group results stated above. P Limited did not sell any goods to Z Limited during the year.
2.	Both companies use the group depreciation policy of 20% per annum on a reducing balance basis for their non-current assets. Neither company made any additions or disposals of non-current assets during the year.

Task

On 10ᵗʰ January 20X1, you receive the following email:

From:	Richard Smithrichardsmith@pzgroup.co.uk
Sent:	10ᵗʰ January, 9.30 a.m.
Subject:	Performance of PZ Group

I am currently putting together the board papers for the January 20X1 board meeting. Graham Tagg is really keen to build up his understanding of the performance and performance measures of the PZ Group. I would like your help with this and have prepared some ratios to assist you (Exhibit 1).

Graham Tagg's previous employer had a very successful transfer pricing policy. He is keen to introduce a similar policy for the PZ Group.

Please could you prepare a report for the January 20X1 board meeting including the following:

- An analysis of the performance of P Limited and Z limited for the year ended 31 December 20X0, paying particular attention to the impact of intragroup transactions on the key ratios of return on capital employed, operating margin and asset turnover.

- Potential disadvantages of using return on capital employed as a measure to determine divisional managers' bonuses.

The main focus of the report should be the analysis of the performance of P Limited and Z Limited.

Kind regards,

Richard

Finance Director

PZ Group

E: richardsmith@pzgroup.co.uk

T: 01225 444123

Prepare the report requested by Richard Smith in the email above.

Exhibit 1

Key ratios for P Limited and Z Limited

Company	P Limited	Z Limited
Return on capital employed (using profit before interest and tax)	4.4%	6.6%
Operating profit margin	10.0%	13.6%
Asset turnover	0.44	0.49

Exhibit 2

Impact of intragroup sales on ratios

Gross margins of Z Limited

Z Limited	Gross margin
On internal sales	50%
On external sales	25%

Gross margins of P Limited

P Limited	Gross margin
On external sales	14%

Amended ratios of P Limited and Z Limited with impact of intragroup transactions removed

Company	P Limited	Z Limited
Return on capital employed (using profit before interest and tax)	3.6%	4.4%
Operating profit margin	9.3%	10.0%
Asset turnover	0.39	0.44

Note: In calculating these ratios, adjustments have been made to remove the intragroup revenue and cost of sales, the intragroup profit and profit arising from P Limited selling the goods purchased from Z Limited on to third parties, because, if P Limited had not purchased the goods from Z Limited, they would not have been able to sell them on to third parties.

END OF TASK

Topic 6 – F2 Primary Tasks Solutions

Task 25

Marking scheme

	Marks
Sub-task 1 - Airport collapse	
Up to 2 marks per relevant well explained point:	Up to 2 each
3 criteria for a provision	
Whether provision criteria have been met	
Definition of a contingent liability	
Whether contingent liability definition has been met	
Conclusion that it is a contingent liability not a provision	
Disclosure requirements for a contingent liability	
Maximum for sub-task 1	**12**
Sub-task 2 - Investment in Bodair	
Up to 2 marks per relevant well explained point:	Up to 2 each
Definition of an associate	
Investment in Bodair – indicators of significant influence:	
• 2 of 10 members of board of directors	
• Unanimous or majority consent required for certain decisions	
• Material transaction between Newnham and Bodair (sale of software licence)	
• Provision of management services	
19.9% deliberate attempt to keep below 20% threshold?	
Investment at cost, as available for sale financial asset or under equity method in individual company financial statements	
Equity account in group financial statements	
Associate = related party	
Disclose related party transactions between Newnham and Bodair	
Maximum for sub-task 2	**13**
MAXIMUM FOR TASK	**25**

Suggested solution

REPORT

To: **Kate Smith**
Date: **15th February 20X1**
Subject: **Accounting treatment for airport collapse and investment in Bodair**

<u>Introduction</u>

This report outlines the accounting treatment for the transactions raised in your email in the financial statements of Newnham for the year ended 31 December 20X0.

The airport collapse

A provision is defined by IAS 37 *Provisions, contingent liabilities and contingent assets* as a liability of uncertain timing or amount. IAS 37 states that a provision should only be recognised if there is all three of:

- A present obligation (legal or constructive) as the result of a past event;
- A probable outflow of resources; and
- A reliable estimate of the amount.

As at 31 December 20X0, although there is a past event in the form the airport collapse, it is not yet obligating as no legal action has been brought in respect of the accident. Therefore, Newnham has no legal obligation to pay compensation to third parties. Nor does Newnham have a constructive obligation at the year end, because the investigation has not been concluded, and the expert report will not be presented to the civil courts until 20X1. Therefore under IAS 37, no provision would be recognised for legal compensation and damages.

However, the possible payment does fall within the IAS 37 definition of a contingent liability:

- A possible obligation depending on whether some uncertain future event occurs, or

- A present obligation but payment is not probable or the amount cannot be measured reliably.

There is uncertainty as to the outcome of the investigation and findings of the report, and the extent of the damages and any compensation arising remain to be confirmed. Therefore, there is a possible obligation. Furthermore, the uncertainty over these details is not so great that the possibility of an outflow of economic benefits is remote. Therefore, a contingent liability exists.

Whilst you are correct that no provision should be made, it would be incorrect not to disclose a contingent liability in a note to the financial statements. Therefore, we must disclose a brief description of the contingent liability, an estimate of the financial effect, an indication of the uncertainties relating to the amount and timing of any outflow and the possibility of any reimbursement.

Investment in Bodair

Associate

In accounting for Bodair, IAS 28 *Investments in associates and joint ventures* must be considered. IAS 28 defines an associate as 'an entity in which an investor has significant influence but not control or joint control'.

Significant influence is the power to participate in the financial and operating policy decisions, but is not control or joint control over those policies. It can be determined by the holding of voting rights (usually attached to shares) in the entity. IAS 28 states that if an investor holds 20% or more of the voting power of the investee, it can be presumed that the investor has significant influence over the investee, *unless* it can be clearly shown that this is not the case.

Significant influence can be presumed *not* to exist if the investor holds less than 20% of the voting power of the investee, unless it can be demonstrated otherwise.

Newnham might be perceived to be holding 19.9% of the voting shares of Bodair in a deliberate attempt to keep just below the threshold at which significant influence would be presumed, in order to avoid accounting for Bodair as an associate. The percentage of shares held is only one factor to consider, and IAS 28 requires other factors to be considered:

(i) Representation on the board of directors– Newnham has representation on Bodair's board of directors (two of the ten directors);

(ii) Participation in the policy making process – Newnham can participate to some extent as the shareholders' agreement requires a unanimous or majority decision;

(iii) Material transactions between the entity and investee – during the year Newnham sold Bodair a software licence for $5 million;

(iv) Interchange of management personnel – there is no evidence of this;

(v) Provision of essential technical information – Newnham provided Bodair with business advice.

As so many indicators of significant influence appear to be present and the holding is only just under the 20% threshold, it appears that Newnham does have significant influence over Bodair. Accordingly, IAS 28 applies and Bodair must be treated as an associate.

Your proposed accounting treatment of recording the shares in Bodair as an available for sale investment is allowed in the individual financial statements of Newnham as IAS 27 *Separate financial statements* permits an investment in an associate in the parent's financial statements to be held at cost, in accordance with IAS 39 *Financial instruments: recognition and measurement* or using the equity method. However, it is not permitted in the group financial statements, where Bodair must be equity accounted as an associate.

Related party disclosures

As an associate, Bodair is a related party of Newnham under IAS 24 *Related party disclosures.* IAS 24 requires disclosure in the financial statements of Newnham of the related party relationship between Newnham and Bodair and also of transactions between the two companies, the total value of those transactions and outstanding balances and, if applicable, debts deemed irrecoverable. Therefore, the sale of the software licence and the business advice must be disclosed.

Conclusion

I hope the above explanations of the accounting treatment are clear. Please do get in contact if you have any queries.

Competency coverage

Sub Task	Technical		Business acumen		People		Leadership		Integration		Max
1	Accounting treatment for airport collapse	12									12
2	Accounting treatment for investment in Bodair	13									13
Total		25									25

Task 26

Marking scheme

	Marks

Sub-task 1 – Accounting treatment for planned disposals

Up to 2 marks per well explained point: — Up to 2 each

Disposal of shares in AB:

- Consol SPLOCI – consolidate up to disposal date (pro-rate if mid-year)
- Consol SOFP – do not consolidate (assuming sold by year end)
- Record group profit on disposal in profit or loss

Disposal of shares in CD:

- Substance – not a disposal as still retain controlling interest & still a subsidiary
- Treat as a transaction between group shareholders
- Consol SPLOCI – consol a full year & pro-rate NCI
- Consol SOFP – consolidate (still a subsidiary at the year end)
- Increase NCI in consol SOFP & record adjustment to parent's equity

Maximum for sub-task 1 — **15**

Sub-task 2 – Impact of disposals on earnings and share price

Up to 2 marks per well explained point: — Up to 2 each

AB

- Fall in overall group earnings
- Increase in group gross & net margins
- Likely increase in share price

CD:

- Minimal effect on earnings
- Possible adverse impact on share price

Maximum for sub-task 2 — <u>10</u>

MAXIMUM FOR TASK — <u>25</u>

Suggested solution

BRIEFING NOTE

To: **Sam Waddon**
Date: **18 August 20X9**
Subject: **Accounting treatment for planned disposals and acquisition**

Introduction

This briefing document explains how to account for the planned disposals in MT group's consolidated financial statements for the year ended 30 June 20X6 and the potential impact on earnings and share price.

(i)   Accounting treatment

Disposal of shares in AB

The proposal is to dispose of all the shares in AB. Assuming the disposal takes place in the year ended 30 June 20X6, the results of AB will be consolidated in the group statement of profit or loss and other comprehensive income, time-apportioned up to the disposal date. A group profit or loss on disposal should be calculated as the consideration received (i.e. the sales proceeds) less the consolidated carrying value (i.e. net assets plus goodwill less non-controlling interests). As the profit or loss on disposal is likely to be material, it should be shown on the face of the consolidated statement of profit or loss and other comprehensive income.

As the shares will no longer be owned at the year end, AB will not be included in the consolidated statement of financial position of the MT group.

Disposal of shares in CD

As a controlling shareholding will be retained in CD, the income and expenses of CD must be consolidated for the full year in the group consolidated statement of profit or loss and other comprehensive income. However, the disposal of shares will cause an increase in the non-controlling interest. Therefore, non-controlling interest (NCI) in profit for the year (PFY) and total comprehensive income (TCI) must be time-apportioned with amounts up to the disposal date (multiplied by the NCI percentage prior to the disposal i.e. 25%) and amounts from the disposal to the year end (multiplied by the NCI percentage after the disposal i.e. 35%).

In substance, as MT will retain a controlling interest, there will have been no disposal. Instead it must be treated as a transaction between group shareholders, with the parent (MT) selling shares to the non-controlling interests. As such, it should be reported in equity in the consolidated statement of financial position, with:

*   An increase in non-controlling interest, and

*   An adjustment to the parent's (MT's) equity, calculated as the consideration received (i.e. sales proceeds) less the increase in the NCI.

(ii) Impact on earnings and share price

As profit figures for the year ended 30 June 20X6 and the exact date of the planned disposals and acquisition are unknown, approximate estimates of the impact on earnings are based on profit figures for the year ended 30 June 20X5.

If the full shareholding in AB had been disposed of in the year ended 30 June 20X5, group earnings would have been approximately $81 million lower (i.e. $90 million profit for the year multiplied by 90% shareholding). However, as AB has a lower gross margin that the rest of the MT group (33% as opposed to 40%) and a lower net margin (6% as opposed to 7.5%), although in absolute terms group earnings will fall, the group gross and net margins will increase. Given the negative publicity in relation to AB's products (fruit-based alcoholic cocktails), despite the fall in earnings, disposal of AB is likely to be viewed positively by the market, resulting in an increase in share price.

The disposal of shares in CD will have a minimal effect on earnings as MT is retaining a controlling stake and will still need to consolidate CD. However, as the group shareholding is falling, the profit attributable to the owners of MT will also fall. Based on the profit for the year ended 30 June 20X5, profit attributable to the owners of the parent would fall from $75 million to $65 million. There could also be an adverse impact on MT's share price as MT will still be retaining a controlling interest in an entity not considered to be a strategic fit with MT's core values.

Conclusion

This briefing paper has explained the potential accounting treatment for the planned disposals in the group financial statements of the MT group for the year ended 30 June 20X6 and the possible impact on earnings and share price. More detail can be added once the exact date of the disposals has been determined. Please contact me if you have any queries.

Competency coverage

Sub Task	Technical		Business acumen		People		Leadership		Integration		Max
1	Accounting treatment for planned disposals	15									15
2	Impact of disposals on earnings and share price	10									10
Total		25									25

Task 27

Marking scheme

	Marks	Marks

Sub-task 1 - Analysis of financial performance
Award 2 marks per relevant point that explains reason for movement in ratio/balance:

- Growth
- Margins
- Efficiency
- Interest
- Impact of associate

Maximum for sub-task 1 — **10**

Sub-task 2 - Analysis of financial position, non-financial aspects, conclusion
Award 2 marks per relevant point that explains reason for movement in ratio/balance:

- Liquidity
- Gearing
- Working capital management
- Available for sale investment

	Marks	Marks
Maximum for financial position	8	
Non-financial aspects	4	
Conclusion addressing the investment decision	2	
Maximum for sub task 2		**14**

Sub-task 3 - Disadvantages to PaperGlo of listing
Award 2 marks per disadvantage specifically tailored to PaperGlo
Dilution of family control
Pressure from institutional investors
Market pressure
Increase in accountability
Costs

		Marks
Maximum for task 3		**10**
MAXIMUM FOR TASK		**34**

Suggested solution

Task

To:	**Guy Jackman**
Date:	**12th April 20X5**
Subject:	**Analysis of Biggle and disadvantages of listing**

<u>Introduction</u>

These notes:

- Analyse the financial performance of Biggle;
- Analyse the financial position of Biggle; and
- Explain potential disadvantages to PaperGlo of listing.

<u>Analysis of Biggle</u>

Financial performance

Growth

The increase in revenue of 40% is due to the expansion into new markets (domestic supermarkets in New Zealand and a European supermarket chain).

Margins

The expansion seems to have been at the expense of profitability. The gross margin has fallen from 31% to 26%, presumably due to the supermarkets negotiating a lower sales price. Supermarkets are renowned for placing aggressive price pressure on suppliers.

Once the impact of the associate is removed, the operating margin has fallen by marginally more than the gross margin, largely due to a 58% increase in distribution costs, presumably as a result of selling to the overseas European supermarket chain.

The decrease could also be from the purchase of new machinery in the year, resulting in higher depreciation charges. The low carbon footprint of these new assets is aligned with PaperGlo's strategy of environmental excellence. Depreciation has also increased due to the revaluation of non-current assets in the year.

The chairman's announcement of increased profit is based on figures including the share of the profits of an associate acquired during the year. Excluding the results of the associate, the profit before tax has decreased from NZ$125 million to NZ$80 million, partly due to the fall in gross and operating margins but also to the doubling of the finance cost in the year as a result of an overdraft in the current year and an increase in long-term borrowings.

However, the associate has been a wise investment, generating a return of approximately 45%.

Efficiency

Non-current asset turnover has increased from 2.5 to 3.0 which is impressive given that the assets were revalued in the year. This suggests that the company is making effective use of the new non-current assets to increase revenue.

Financial position

Liquidity

The quick ratio has fallen from 2.3 to 1.8, largely due to a positive cash balance of NZ$22m in 20X3 becoming an overdraft of NZ$37m in 20X4. This is as a result of the expansion and poor working capital management (see below).

Gearing

Gearing has increased from 43% to 66% because the company is becoming heavily reliant on borrowings. Loans have nearly doubled and Biggle now has an overdraft. Presumably this new finance was raised to fund the expansion. Biggle appears to be relying on the overdraft as a long term source of finance which is both expensive and risky.

Working capital

Working capital management has deteriorated, possibly as a result of the expansion. Inventory days have increased from 34 to 50 days, which is tying up cash. Receivables days have increased from 48 to 63 days. This is likely to be due to the new customers (supermarkets) demanding longer credit terms and potentially not adhering to those credit terms. This could indicate a need to tighten up credit control.

Payable days have remained static. Payables are being paid more quickly than cash is being collected from customers, which is not sustainable in the long term. All of the above are causing liquidity problems.

Available for sale investment

This investment has increased in value by $10m in the year, indicating strong treasury management.

Non-financial aspects

If PaperGlo were to acquire Biggle, PaperGlo would be forced to increase its carbon footprint and transport costs by purchasing all raw materials from Biggle's manufacturing facility (based in New Zealand rather than Australia).

There is also some doubt about whether Biggle would be a good strategic fit given that its growth appears to be predominantly in the supermarket sector, whose sustainability credentials are questionable.

Care would also have to be taken with the supply chain for sales to new customers based in New Zealand. Rather than shipping supplies from New Zealand to PaperGlo in Australia then back again to customers in New Zealand, to preserve our carbon footprint, goods would need to be delivered directly from Biggle's manufacturing facilities to customers. Biggle's new contract with the European supermarket chain would also cause PaperGlo's carbon footprint to increase.

Further investigation also needs to be made into the associate to ensure that it is a good strategic fit in terms of sustainability.

Finally, there is a risk that acquisition of Biggle by PaperGlo could result in Biggle losing customers if PaperGlo is perceived to be in direct competition with Biggle's customers as it operates in the same market (stationery retail).

Conclusion

Arguments in favour of investing in Biggle include the 40% increase in revenue, from new domestic and overseas customers, and a $28m increase in profit, largely due to the investment in the associate in the year.

However, the growth in revenue has been at the cost of profitability. Once the associate is removed from the results, profit margins have declined. The expansion has also been at the cost of liquidity with Biggle suffering from poor working capital management and a large overdraft. The investment would be risky, too, as Biggle is highly geared.

Finally, there is a risk of damage to our sustainability ethos.

These reservations must be addressed before a final investment decision is made.

Disadvantages to PaperGlo of listing

Dilution of power

Currently, Pete Watts and his family retain a controlling interest in PaperGlo. If PaperGlo lists on the securities exchange, this will attract investment from new external investors. There is a risk that the family lose their controlling interest and therefore, their decision-making power over the business.

Institutional investors

If the investors are large institutional ones, they are likely to have more exacting requirements than the existing shareholders. They will probably seek to have considerable involvement in running PaperGlo and may wish to influence the remuneration of the board.

Market pressure

There is also a risk of market pressure for growth and increased profitability which risks damaging PaperGlo's core ethos of sustainability.

Increased accountability

There would be the increase in public regulation, accountability and scrutiny. The legal requirements PaperGlo will face will be greater and the company will be subject to the rules of the Australian Securities Exchange.

Costs

There will be additional costs involved in making future share issues, including brokerage commissions and underwriting fees.

Competency coverage

Sub Task	Technical		Business acumen		People		Leadership		Integration		Max
1	Analysis of financial performance	10									10
2	Analysis of financial position, non-financial aspects, conclusion	14									14
3	Disadvantages to PaperGlo of listing	10									10
Total		34									34

Task 28

Marking scheme

	Marks	Marks
Sub-task 1 – Change in management style following the acquisition by SW Group		
Current approach (up to 2 marks per relevant, well-explained point), up to max of	2	
Likely future approach (up to 2 marks per relevant, well-explained point), up to max of	9	
Maximum for sub-task 1		11

	Marks	Marks
Sub-task 2 – Functional currency of T Company and translation for group accounts		
Up to 2 marks per relevant, well-explained point:	Up to 2 each	
Definition of functional currency (IAS 21)		
Application of factors for identifying functional currency to scenario:		
• Currency of sales = T$ as sales to customers in T-Land		
• Senior management likely to be from SW Group & paid in A$ but majority of T Company's employees will be retained & paid in T$		
• Purchases locally – therefore in T$		
• Even though senior management from SW Group, T Company will continue to operate largely independently		
• Anticipated that cash flows of T Company will be sufficient to service debt		
Conclusion that functional currency of T Company = T$		
SOFP: translate assets and liabilities @ closing rate		
SPLOCI: translate income and expenses @ actual or average rate		
Goodwill: translate @ closing rate		
Exchange differences: to other comprehensive income & translation reserve		
Maximum for sub-task 2		12
Integration marks		2
MAXIMUM FOR TASK		25

Suggested solution

BRIEFING NOTE

To: Z
Date: 5th October 20X5
Subject: Management style of T Company and inclusion of T Company in the consolidated financial statements of SW Group

Introduction

This briefing note addresses:

• The likely change in management style of T Company as a result of the acquisition by SW Group

- The functional currency of T Company and how to translate the financial statements of T Company for inclusion in the consolidated financial statements of SW Group.

Management style

Current approach

The current approach is very participative, with all employees contributing in some way to the day-to-day running of the business. Staff members are encouraged to contribute new ideas to aid in decision making and local knowledge is valued. In return, staff have developed a flexible approach to their roles within the company to ensure that business needs are met. This is in line with a task culture.

The approach is consistent with Mayo's human relations school of management theory as the social aspect of work appears to be motivating the employees and the owner/manager takes a personal interest in each member of staff.

Likely future approach

It is expected that the acquisition will lead to the implementation of a much more bureaucratic approach ie more formal and standardised than the current approach.

The culture is likely to move away from the existing task culture towards more of a role culture reflecting the shift in power that will have occurred.

Operational staff would no longer be involved in decision making or encouraged to contribute their ideas. Instead, strategy would be developed at the top and imposed down on the rest of the organisation. This is a major cultural change for the staff which it may find difficult to adapt to.

Job roles and responsibilities will be much more standardised in a bureaucratic management approach and the current flexibility between the roles will be greatly reduced. Clear chains of command between the roles will also be established. This will lead to a clear division of labour with duties and authority levels formalised.

The responsibility hierarchy that has been created is likely to cause the speed of communication within the organisation to slow down as communication and coordination will become the management's responsibility. Communication will then occur through more structured and defined channels. This is likely to cause a degree of frustration among existing T Company staff.

The current informal relationships between the employees and the managers are also likely to change under this new approach to become more formal. Employees at T Company may also experience "personality clashes" because not only is it likely that business will be conducted in a different way, but also that the prevailing culture in A Land will impact the way that people communicate with each other or their working hours, for example.

The likely changes at T Company are significant and will have a major impact on the working lives of the T Company employees. Many staff have remained with T Company for a long time and have worked their way up through the organisation. For these staff, and others that have spent a significant proportion of their working lives at T Company, the transition is likely to be very difficult.

Inclusion of T Company in the consolidated financial statements of SW Group

Functional currency

The functional currency is defined by IAS 21 as 'the currency of the primary economic environment in which the entity operates'.

Factors to consider include:

(i) The currency that mainly influences sales prices: This will continue to be T$ as sales will continue to be made to customers in T-Land.

(ii) The currency of the country whose competitive forces and regulations mainly determine sales prices: This will continue to be T$, as the company will continue to be based in T-Land and therefore subject to market forces and regulations in that country.

(iii) The currency that mainly influences labour, material and other costs: Whilst the new senior management team will come from SW Group and may be paid in their currency (A$), the majority of existing T Company employees will be retained and paid in T$. As goods will continue to be purchased locally, these will be paid in T$.

(iv) Whether the activities of the foreign subsidiary are carried out as an extension of the reporting entity, rather than with a significant degree of autonomy: Even though the senior management team of T Company will comprise employees from SW Group, T Company will continue to operate largely independently, implying that the functional currency is T$ rather that A$.

(v) Whether transactions with the reporting entity are a high or low proportion of the foreign subsidiary's activities: Post acquisition, the level of intragroup transactions between T Company and SW group is anticipated to be low, implying that the functional currency is T$.

(vi) Whether cash flows from the activities of the foreign subsidiary are sufficient to service its debt obligations: It is anticipated that the cash flows of T Company will be sufficient to service its own debt, indicating that the functional currency is T$.

(vii) Whether cash flows from the activities of the foreign subsidiary directly affect the cash flows of the parent and are readily available for remittance to it: Given the low level of intragroup transactions, and the autonomy that T Company is expected to have, T Company's cash flows are unlikely to directly affect the cash flows of SW. This is another indication that the functional currency is T$.

The above factors indicate that the primary economic environment of T Company post-acquisition will continue to be T-Land. Therefore, T Company's functional currency should be T$.

Inclusion in the consolidated financial statements of SW Group

T Company will need to translate its financial statements from T$ into A$ for consolidation purposes.

Assets and liabilities should be translated at the closing rate. Income and expenses should be translated at the actual rate but the average rate can be used as a close approximation.

Any goodwill arising on acquisition of T Company by SW Group should be translated at the closing rate.

Exchange differences will arise on retranslation of opening net assets, profit and goodwill. These should be reported in other comprehensive income and a translation reserve.

Conclusion

I hope the above assists you in preparation for your discussions with employees. If you would like any further help, please let me know.

Competency coverage

Sub Task	Technical		Business acumen		People		Leadership		Integration		Max
1			E2 - Change in management style following acquisition by SW Group	11							11
2	F2 - Inclusion of T Company in consolidated financial statements of SW Group	12									12
Total		12		11						2	25

Task 29

Marking scheme

	Marks	Marks
MEMORANDUM		
Sub-task 1 – Share-based payment		
Up to 2 marks per valid well-explained point		
Accounting treatment		
Types		
Recognition:		
Ethical implication of not recognising an expense		
Measurement		
Up to a max of:	7	
Market preference		
Choice and reason why		
Up to a max of:	<u>2</u>	
Maximum for sub-task 1		9
Sub-task 2 – Distinction between financial control and treasury functions and interaction		
Up to 2 marks per valid well-explained point		
Financial control function in context of MiniMark Co		
Treasury function in context of MiniMark Co		
Interaction between the two functions		
Maximum for sub-task 2		6
Sub-task 3 – Use of balanced scorecard to assess finance function		
Application of each quadrant to MiniMark Co's financial control department (2 marks per quadrant):		
Customers		
Internal processes		
Financial		
Innovation and learning		
Maximum for sub-task 3		8
Integration marks		<u>2</u>
MAXIMUM FOR TASK		<u>25</u>

Suggested solution

MEMORANDUM

To: **Douglas Wallis**
Date: **18th January 20X7**
Subject: **Share-based payments, treasury and financial control departments and balanced scorecard**

<u>Introduction</u>

This memorandum:

(i) Explains how the directors' bonus would be accounted for if it were a share-based payment.

(ii) Distinguishes the financial control function from the treasury function, identifying any areas of interaction.

(iii) Explains the ways in which the balanced scorecard approach could be used in appraising the finance function.

(i) <u>Share-based payment</u>

Types

IFRS 2 covers two different types of share-based payment:

- Equity-settled - an entity receives goods or services for its own equity instruments (eg share options);

- Cash-settled - an entity acquires goods or services by incurring a liability to transfer cash, based on the price of equity instruments (eg share-appreciation rights where the amount of cash is based on the increase in share price).

Recognition

Share-based payments to employees are usually conditional on the staff remaining in employment for a specified period (the 'vesting period').

IFRS 2 requires an expense to be recognised for the share-based payment because when granted to employees, the share-based payment is effectively a payment for the employees' services (ie a form of remuneration). Even if the share-based payment is a share option and no cash is paid, an expense must still be recognised.

We need to explain to Douglas Wallis that failure to record an expense would result in non-compliance with IFRS 2 and potential ethical implications because the CIMA Code of Ethics requires an accountant to demonstrate the principle of professional competence.

To match the benefits generated by employees working for the company, the expense must be spread over the vesting period.

The other side of the accounting entry depends on the type of share-based payment:

- Equity-settled - credit equity (usually 'other reserves');

- Cash-settled - credit liabilities, as the entity has an obligation to pay the cash to employees when the instruments vest.

Measurement

Ideally, the direct method should be used (ie the fair value of goods or services received). However, for share-based payments made to employees, it is difficult to measure reliably the value of employee services received, so instead, the indirect method is used whereby the amount is measured at the fair value of the share-based payment.

For equity-settled share-based payments, the fair value at the grant date is used. No adjustment should be made to this fair value in subsequent years.

For cash-settled share-based payments, the fair value is updated each year end to ensure that the best estimate of what the entity is likely to pay is recognised.

The value of the share-based payment equity or liability should be updated each year end to reflect the estimated number of employees entitled to receive the share-based payment.

Market preference

The market is likely to react more positively to a share-based payment than immediate cash bonuses as payment is deferred. An equity-settled share-based payment would probably be preferred to a cash-settled one as it would result in no cash outflow from MiniMark Co to employees. The market would only view a share-based payment positively if it were conditional on future employment. Otherwise, it would be likely to encourage short-termism, with the employee aiming to maximise profits in the short term rather than acting in the longer term interest of shareholders.

(ii)   <u>The finance and treasury functions</u>

Financial control involves the allocation and effective use of resources, including advising on performance and investment appraisal opportunities as well as reporting on results. For MiniMark Co, the financial control function would report on branch performance and advise on the viability (or otherwise) of new or existing branches.

The treasury function is involved in obtaining suitable types of finance, including advising on sources of finance and dividend policy, as well as hedging to manage risk and liaising with financial stakeholders (such as banks and key shareholders). As a listed company, it is important that MiniMark Co's dividend policy is clearly communicated to stakeholders and is financially viable.

A large organisation like MiniMark Co would normally separate these two functions. Nevertheless, they would work closely together. For example, the treasury function would provide a cost of capital for the financial control function to assess the viability of a potential new project. Furthermore, the financial control function would report on the impact of currency risk, while the treasury department would be responsible for managing that risk through hedging.

(iii)   <u>How the balanced scorecard approach could be used to appraise the financial control function</u>

The balanced scorecard categorises performance measures under four headings. By using all four headings, a more rounded measure of the function's effectiveness can be gained.

- **Customers.** The financial control function's customers are the internal departments in MiniMark. Do these stakeholders get the information they need in a user-friendly format and a timely manner? This would apply to monthly performance reports and ad hoc investment appraisals (eg an analysis of the viability of a new or existing store).

- **Internal processes.** Are the processes sufficiently robust to allow timely, accurate delivery of information? Internal stakeholders should expect monthly performance reviews within 1 – 2 weeks of the month end. The systems would need to be robust enough to allow ad hoc requests for information to be extracted efficiently.

- **Financial.** Is the financial control department financially viable in itself? Is it creating value for the company? This could be ascertained through an internal transfer pricing policy. Although the value generated by the department may be difficult to measure, it should provide its service more cheaply and effectively than an outsource provider.

- **Innovation and learning**. Does the financial control function train its staff in order to improve levels of service? For example, staff may be training in a professional accountancy qualification, or in new IT systems (such as Big Data) to allow internal data to be harnessed to maximum effect.

Having considered these issues, a series of specific measures would need to be set for each heading. For example, to demonstrate appropriate internal processes, the monthly accounts will be expected within X working days of the month end.

Conclusion

I hope this report helps to clarify the accounting treatment for share-based payments, the roles of the treasury and financial control departments and how MiniMark Co could use the balanced scorecard approach. The Finance Director and Financial Controller would be happy to answer any queries.

Competency coverage

Sub Task	Technical		Business acumen		People		Leadership		Integration		Max
1	F2 - Share-based payment: accounting treatment and market preference	9									9
2			E2 - Distinction between financial control and treasury functions and interaction	6							6
3			Use of balanced scorecard to assess finance function	8							8
Total		9		14						2	25

BPP LEARNING MEDIA

Task 30

Marking scheme

Sub-task 1 – Analysis of performance of P Limited and Z Limited
Award 2 marks per relevant well-explained point (to maximum of 15 marks):
Volume of business – similar once intragroup sales stripped out
Margins:
- Intragoup sales at higher gross margin that external sales
- Once strip out intragroup sales, similar operating margins
- Z limited better gross margin on external sales
- P limited better at controlling overheads

Return on capital employed:
- Z Limited's ROCE higher than P Limited's (even after removing intragroup)
- Z Limited's assets cost more than P Limited's but older so lower carrying amount

Asset turnover:
- Z Limited seems more efficient at generating revenue from assets
- But distorted by Z Limited having older assets

Gearing:
- P Limited's profit before tax is one third of Z Limited's
- Different capital structures - P Limited has long-term borrowings; Z Limited has none – P's higher interest helps explain lower profit
- P Limited more risky – interest = non-discretionary; dividends discretionary

Conclusion
Maximum for sub-task 1   **15**

Sub-task 2 – Disadvantages of using ROCE to determine bonuses
Award 2 marks per relevant well-explained point (to maximum of 8 marks):
Demotivation: bonus measured on ratio impacted by factors beyond their control
Not useful where decisions made centrally
Incentive to over-report income and under-report costs/creative accounting
Divisions in different geographical regions: risk of different cost-bases
Maximum for sub-task 2   **8**
Integration marks $\underline{2}$
MAXIMUM FOR TASK $\underline{\underline{25}}$

Suggested solution

REPORT

To: **Directors of the PZ Group**

Date: **15th January 20X1**

Subject: **Performance of P Limited and Z Limited and risks of using return on capital employed to determine bonuses**

<u>Introduction</u>

This board paper includes:

- An analysis of the performance of P Limited and Z Limited for the year ended 31 December 20X0, paying particular attention to the impact of intragroup transactions on key ratios; and

- Disadvantages of using return on capital employed as a measure to determine divisional managers' bonuses.

(i)   <u>Performance of P Limited and Z Limited</u>

Volume of business

At first it appears as if Z Limited has sold more goods that P Limited. However, Z Limited's revenue is artificially inflated by $20 million of intragroup sales. This amount can be calculated by comparing the group revenue against the sum of the individual company revenue figures since intragroup transactions are eliminated on consolidation ([$200 million + $220 million] – $400 million).

Once this intragroup revenue has been stripped out, it can be seen that the two entities are operating at a similar level.

Margins

The intragroup sales were sold at a higher gross margin than the gross margin on Z Limited's external sales (50% as opposed to 25%).

This helps explain why before stripping out the impact of intragroup sales, Z Limited's operating profit margin (13.6%) is considerably higher than P Limited's operating profit margin (10%). Once the impact of the intragroup sale has been stripped out, including the profit made by P Limited selling the goods on to third parties, the difference between the two entities' operating margin is only 0.7% (10% for Z Limited and 9.3% for P Limited).

This remaining difference in operating margin is partly because Z Limited makes a better gross margin on external sales than P Limited i.e. 25% as opposed to 14%. On the other hand, P Limited is much better at controlling its overheads than Z Limited, with administrative expenses being one third of Z Limited's administrative expenses. This explains why the difference in the operating margin is so small.

Return on capital employed and asset turnover

Removing the impact of intragroup sales also makes return on capital employed more comparable. However, Z Limited's return on capital employed (4.4%) is still better than P Limited's (3.6%), suggesting the Z Limited is able to use the capital at its disposal more efficiently to generate earnings.

225

This is partly due to the age of the two entities' assets. A greater portion of Z Limited's assets have been depreciated than that of P Limited. This implies that Z Limited's assets are older that P Limited's, which, on a reducing balance basis, results in a lower annual depreciation charge and higher profit for Z Limited. This is the case even though Z Limited's assets cost 50% more than P Limited's. This is because the age of the assets makes the carrying amount of Z Limited's assets lower than P Limited's and since a reducing balance depreciation policy is being used, depreciation is charged on this lower carrying amount rather than higher cost.

The lower carrying amount of Z Limited's non-current assets also helps explain why Z Limited's asset turnover is higher than P Limited's.

Profit before tax

P Limited's profit before tax is one third of Z Limited's. As well as being due to a lower gross margin, this is also because P Limited and Z Limited have different capital structures. P Limited has long term borrowings while Z Limited has no borrowings. This means that P Limited has a $10 million finance charge whilst Z Limited has none, thus further reducing P Limited's profit before tax.

This makes P Limited more risky than Z Limited, since in periods of volatile profitability, P Limited might not be able to afford to pay this interest. Interest is a non-discretionary cost whereas dividends are entirely at the discretion of the directors.

Conclusion

Return on capital employed and its two component ratios of operating margin and asset turnover are of limited use when comparing two different entities with different ages of assets and when the distorting effect of intragroup transactions are included.

Also, as profit before interest and tax is used, no account is taken of the two entities' different capital structures and the resulting impact on risk.

(ii) <u>Disadvantages of using return on capital employed (ROCE) to determine bonuses</u>

- Divisional managers may become demotivated when they realise that their bonus is being measured on a ratio impacted by factors beyond their control (e.g. intragroup transactions and age of assets).

- It is not a useful measure where decisions relating to revenue, costs and investments are made centrally, as the divisional managers will not be assessed on their individual performance.

- There is an incentive for divisional managers to over-report income and under-report costs or use creative accounting to maximise ROCE and their resultant bonus.

- If, like P Limited and Z Limited, the divisions are operating in different geographical regions, there is a risk that the cost-base (e.g. employment costs) may be higher in one region than the other, giving the division operating in the lower cost-base an advantage.

<u>Conclusion</u>

I hope that this board paper has been useful. Please direct any queries to the finance department.

Competency coverage

Sub Task	Technical		Business acumen		People		Leadership		Integration		Max
1	F2/P2 – Analysis of performance of P Limited and Z Limited	15									15
2	P2 – disadvantages of using return on capital employed to determine bonuses	8									8
Integration											2
Total		23								2	25

Topic 6 – F2 Further Tasks

Task 31 Dragon Estates

Indicative timing: 45 mins (excluding Background Information)

Background information

Dragon Estates is a property development company based in Asia. Founded seven years ago in Drukeland, Dragon Estates is expanding rapidly. Its expansion has involved numerous high-profile acquisitions of land and buildings throughout Asia Pacific. Dragon Estates prepares its financial statements in accordance with IFRS.

You are Alyssa Chung, and you joined the company a month ago as financial controller. You report to Norman Koh, the Finance Director, who is a CIMA-qualified management accountant and has been on the Board since the founding of Dragon Estates.

During the handover in your first week, your predecessor explained that the company's financial reporting system was 'badly in need of an update' and that, unfortunately, this was 'unlikely to happen any time soon, because the directors consider financial reporting to be just an annoying distraction from their objective of making money.'

Task

As the accounts department is finalising the financial statements of Dragon Estates for the year ended 31 December 20X4, you note two transactions in respect of which you require more information: the sale of a piece of land and the long-term lease of a building. You write a note to the Finance Director inquiring about the transactions.

You receive this email in response:

From:	NormanKoh@dragon.com
To:	AlyssaChung@dragon.com
Sent:	10th February 20X5, 10 am

Subject: Financial statements for year ended 31 December 20X4

Hi Alyssa,

Thank you for your message. I don't blame you for asking questions, especially as you are still fairly new at the company. Both of these transactions precede your time with us.

Sale of land

On 31 May 20X4 Dragon Estates sold a piece of land intended for development to Veetle, a third-party company that provides Dragon Estates with long-term finance. The sale price was $1,600,000 and the carrying value of the land on the date of the sale was $1,310,000 (the original cost of the asset). Under the terms of the sale agreement, Dragon Estates has the option to repurchase the land within the next four years for between $1,660,000 and $1,800,000 depending on the date of repurchase. Veetle cannot use the land for any purpose without the prior consent of Dragon Estates. The land must be repurchased for $1,800,000 at the end of the four year period if the option is not exercised before that time.

Dragon Estates has derecognised the value of the land from inventory and recorded the proceeds from the sale as revenue for the year.

231

Lease of Telecom Tower

On 1 December 20X4, Dragon Estates signed a 15-year lease for the Telecom Tower, just around the corner from our Head Office. Works are currently underway to convert the building into offices for our central administrative functions. I attach extracts from the lease contract for your reference (**Exhibit 1**).

There is an option for us to purchase Telecom Tower at the end of the lease, but the Board is currently undecided as to whether we will take it up as it is quite expensive. On this basis, I believe that it is correct to account for it as an operating lease. This is how it is currently treated in the draft financial statements.

As you know, we're in the process of preparing for a placing on the Stock Exchange, to fund our future expansion plans. To attract institutional investors, we need to ensure that our financial statements show a high level of return on capital employed. As a CIMA-qualified accountant, I'm sure you understand how important this is and I trust you will bear this in mind when finalising the financial statements. It has been twenty years since I sat my last CIMA exam. Your knowledge of financial reporting is more up to date than mine, so I would appreciate your opinion on this matter.

- Please prepare a report that evaluates the accounting treatment that I have outlined above concerning the two transactions, making reference to the relevant international accounting standards where appropriate and any other professional and ethical issues to consider.

Kind regards,

Norman Koh

Finance Director

Dragon Estates

Prepare the memorandum as requested by the Finance Director. (You do not need to provide journal entries for any adjustments.)

Exhibit 1

Extract from lease contract for Telecom Tower

This agreement is made on 1 December 20X4

between:

Flutefry Real Estates ('the Lessor')

and

Dragon Estates Co ('the Lessee')

Date of the commencement of lease: 1 December 20X4

Date of the termination of the lease: 30 November 20Y9

Duration of the lease: 15 years

Monthly lease cost: $10,500

Present value of minimum lease payments over the duration of the lease: $1,890,000

Market value of the building as at 1 December 20X4: $1,880,000

Market value of the land on which the building is built as at 1 December 20X4: $nil.

The Lessee retains the option to purchase the building upon the termination of the lease, for a payment of $650,000.

The Lessee shall not cancel the lease, or otherwise surrender the lease to another third party, before the termination of the lease on 30 November 20Y9.

The Lessee shall bear all responsibility for the maintenance and management of the building for the duration of the lease. The Lessee shall also assume liability arising from any damage to the building during the lease period.

Task 32 Century

Indicative timing – 45 minutes (excluding Background Information)

Background information

Century is a public limited company operating in the pharmaceutical industry. In recent years, it has made a number of investments in other complementary businesses. Century is based in Schwarzland and reports in Schwarz Dollars ('$').

You are Nik Weiler, the Financial Controller of Century, and have been in the role for some time. You report to Florian Thomas, the Finance Director.

Century owns a 90% subsidiary, Hermosa, specialising in beauty and skincare products. Hermosa was acquired on 1 April 20X1. In the past, Hermosa has supplied its products to other subsidiaries within the group, who rebrand the products for external sale. In recent years, however, intragroup sales have reduced significantly – in 20X7, Hermosa sold $200,000 of goods, representing 6% of its revenue, to the group. The Central and South American markets now account for 85% of Hermosa's revenue.

Century has made a number of strategic investments during the year. Details of the investments are as follows:

Investment in Denzyl

Century acquired 90% of the issued ordinary share capital of Denzyl on 1 July 20X7 for $6 million, when the book value of the net assets was $5.8 million. The fair value of these net assets was estimated at $6.8 million at the date of acquisition. The difference between the fair value and book value of the net assets related to depreciable property with a remaining useful life at the date of acquisition of 40 years.

Investment in Formalight

Century acquired 40% of the issued ordinary share capital of Formalight on 1 January 20X7 for $2 million, when the book value of the net assets was $5.5 million. The fair value of these net assets was estimated at $6 million at the date of acquisition. Century exercises significant influence over Formalight's financial and operating policies.

Investment in Ullenvitte

Century acquired 200,000 of the 250,000 $1 ordinary shares of Ullenvitte on 1 May 20X4 for $1,100,000, when the book value of its net assets was $1.25 million. At the date of acquisition, the fair value of the net assets of Ullenvitte was the same as the book value with the exception of property, plant and equipment.

On 1 October 20X7, Century disposed of 20,000 $1 ordinary shares in Ullenvitte for $115,000. The proceeds were debited to cash and credited to retained earnings.

Investment in Blueskye

Century acquired 15% of the issued ordinary share capital of Blueskye on 1 January 20X2 for $1 million. Up until 1 October 20X7, Century did not have any influence over how Blueskye is managed.

On 1 October 20X7, Century acquired a further 40% of issued ordinary share capital for $4.5 million. The fair value of the net assets at 1 October 20X7 was $12 million and on 1 January 20X2 was $8 million. The previously held interest had a fair value on 1 October 20X7 of $1.7 million.

The group policy is to value non-controlling interest at the date of acquisition at the proportionate share of the fair value of the net assets.

234

Task

It is 20 January 20X8, and the finance team is in the process of preparing the consolidated financial statements for the year ended 31 December 20X7.

You receive the following email from Florian Thomas.

From:	ft@century.com
Sent:	20 January 20X8 9.30 a.m.
Subject:	Preparation for board meeting on 25 January 20X8

Hi Nik,

The next board meeting is in five days, and I am due to report to the board concerning how the investments made during the year will be accounted for in the consolidated financial statements for the year ended 31 December 20X7. I prepared a goodwill working for Denzyl (**Exhibit 1**) at the time of the acquisition, and I would like you to review it.

In addition to this, the Board are now considering a reorganisation of Hermosa, our subsidiary.

Hermosa has always been based in Schwarzland, but logistically and tactically, it makes sense for Hermosa to move to South America, where its market is primarily located.

The directors, with the backing of the non-controlling shareholders of Hermosa, plan to move Hermosa's business operations to a new facility in Guatemala at the end of 20X8. Hermosa would then source all raw materials locally, recruit a local workforce and would be subject to local taxes and corporate regulations. The local currency is the Guatemalan Quetzal (GTQ).

Since acquisition, Hermosa has operated relatively autonomously within the group and this is expected to continue if the move takes place.

The directors need to be briefed on the financial reporting consequences of the relocation at the board meeting. I would like you to prepare notes for me in an email, explaining (with reference to relevant accounting standards to support your argument):

(1)   How each of the investments acquired during the year should be accounted for in the consolidated financial statements of the Century Group for the year ended 31 December 20X7 (calculations are not required). For the investment in Denzyl, please also make reference to my goodwill working.

And more briefly:

(2)   Which currency should be used to prepare the financial statements of Hermosa for the year ended 31 December 20X9, and

(3)   How the financial statements (statement of financial position and statement of profit or loss) of Hermosa should be translated into $s for the consolidated financial statements for the year ended 31 December 20X9.

Thank you.

Kind regards,

FT

Respond to Florian Thomas' email.

Exhibit 1

Denzyl – Goodwill	$'000	$'000
Consideration transferred		6,000
Non-controlling interests (10% × 6,800)		680
		6,680
Less: fair value of net assets		
Book value	5,800	
Fair value adjustment (6,800 – 5,800)	1,000	
		(6,800)
Goodwill		(120)

Task 33 Boson

Indicative timing – 45 minutes (excluding Background Information)

Background information

Boson is a successful listed entity that designs and markets mobile electronic devices. Boson's directors have decided to adopt a policy of expansion into overseas territories through the acquisition of similar software businesses possessing established shares of their domestic markets.

You are Pete Bohr, a senior accountant in Boson's Finance department. You report to Rachel Higgs, the company's Chief Financial Officer (CFO).

The Board of Boson have decided to adopt a strategy of expansion by acquisition, to grow the business's market share overseas. Fermion, a competitor, is currently being considered as an acquisition target.

Fermion's Half-hearted Spin

1 April 20X2

Fermion, the Indian technology company listed on the NSE (National Stock Exchange of India), has thus far held its own in a highly competitive market. Some analysts now question whether it can continue to do so for long. Quark, the newcomer who bounded into the market in 20X1, has put competitive pressure on technology companies by developing marginally lower quality products and selling them at bargain prices. The impact of this can be observed Fermion's latest financial results.

Fermion's share price had fallen significantly in recent months, due partly to a downturn in NSE and partly to the poor interim results that Fermion posted in November 20X1. The share price recovered slightly following the announcement of a final dividend shortly before the year-end. The share price at 31 March 20X2 was $2.50 ($4.34 at 31 March 20X1).

The company's earnings per share for 20X2 was 40c (20X1: 70c). Its PE ratio at 31 March 20X2 was 6.25 (6.20 at 31 March 20X1).

FERMION CO

CONSOLIDATED STATEMENT OF FINANCIAL POSITION AT 31 MARCH

	20X2 $m	20X1 $m
ASSETS		
Non-current assets		
Property, plant and equipment	393	353
Investment in associate	21	24
	414	377
Current assets		
Inventories	210	110
Trade and other receivables	118	103
Cash and cash equivalents	–	24
	328	237
Total assets	742	614
EQUITY AND LIABILITIES		
Equity attributable to owners of the parent		
Share capital ($1 shares)	20	20
Share premium	67	67
Revaluation reserve (Note 4)	20	–
Retained earnings (Note 3)	278	298
	385	385
Non-controlling interest	24	19
Total equity	409	404
Non-current liabilities		
Long-term borrowings (Note 1)	90	90
Current liabilities		
Trade and other payables	196	120
Short-term borrowings (Note 2)	47	–
	243	120
Total liabilities	333	210
Total equity and liabilities	742	614

CONSOLIDATED STATEMENT OF PROFIT OR LOSS AND OTHER COMPREHENSIVE
INCOME FOR THE YEAR ENDED 31 MARCH

	20X2 $m	20X1 $m
Revenue	678	618
Cost of sales	(458)	(402)
Gross profit	220	216
Operating expenses	(185)	(186)
Finance costs	(19)	(8)
Share of (loss)/profit of associate	(2)	2
Profit before tax	14	24
Income tax expense	(3)	(7)
Profit for the year	11	17
Other comprehensive income (not reclassified to profit or loss)		
Revaluation gains from property (net of tax) (Note 4)	20	–
Total comprehensive income	31	17
Profit for the year attributable to:		
Owners of the parent	8	14
Non-controlling interest	3	3
	11	17
Total comprehensive income attributable to:		
Owners of the parent	23	14
Non-controlling interest	8	3
	31	17

Notes

(1)   The long-term borrowings are repayable in 20X5.

(2)   Fermion has a facility in place permitting short-term borrowings up to a maximum of $50 million.

(3)   Fermion and its subsidiary both paid a dividend in the year.

(4)   Fermion changed its group policy on Property, plant and equipment in the year to 31 March 20X2 and now hold these assets at valuation.

Task

You arrive at work on a Monday morning after a long weekend break, and receive this email from Rachel Higgs:

From: rachel.higgs@boson.com
Sent: 20th May 20X2 9.30 a.m.
Subject: Investment plans

Hi Pete,

I hope you had a nice weekend.

As you know, we're looking to expand the business by acquiring competitors with good market prospects. To this end, I would like your help in establishing a set of key accounting ratios for use in:

(1)   the initial appraisal of potential acquisitions;
(2)   on-going appraisal following acquisitions.

Last Friday, in your absence, I asked Polly Tomič, our new Finance assistant, to do some research into the ratios that we can use to this purpose. She suggested two key accounting ratios, as follows:

(1)   Dividend yield: This ratio provides a very useful measurement that allows comparison with yields from other equity and non-equity investments.

(2)   Asset turnover ratios: Allow the investor to compare the intensity of asset usage between businesses, and over time.

One of our acquisition targets, which the CEO is quite keen on, is Fermion, a company based in India. I believe you have already seen a newspaper article about this company, as well as its latest set of financial statements. I now attach some financial ratios which have been provided by our financial advisor (**Exhibit 1**).

The board wants a financial assessment of Fermion's suitability as an acquisition target and I'm due to report to them on this tomorrow. Please could you draft a board report that:

(a)   Explains each of the ratios recommended by Polly, and discusses the extent to which each suggested accounting ratio is likely to be useful to Boson for both initial and on-going appraisal and comparison,

(b)   Analyses in some detail the financial performance and financial position of Fermion and makes a recommendation as to Fermion's suitability for investment based upon the information available, and

(c)   Briefly highlights what post year-end information might be available that would provide us with additional information before we make an investment decision.

Many thanks.

Rachel

Rachel Higgs

CFO

Respond to Rachel Higg's email.

Exhibit 1

Fermion: Financial ratios

	20X2	20X1
Gross margin	32.4%	35.0%
Operating margin	5.2%	4.9%
Quick ratio	0.49	1.06
Inventory days	167 days	100 days
Receivable days	64 days	61 days
Payable days	156 days	109 days

Note: The above ratios do not take into account Fermion's associate.

Task 34 FGH

Indicative timing – 45 minutes (excluding Background Information)

Background information

FGH is a listed entity operating in the manufacturing sector and has been trading for a number of years. FGH is currently going through a period of expansion of its core business area.

You are a member of the accounts department.

The statement of cash flows for the year ended 31 December 20X0 has just been prepared.

FGH Group: Consolidated statement of cash flows for the year ended 31 December 20X0

	$'000	$'000
Cash flows from operating activities		
Profit before taxation	2,200	
Adjustments for:		
Depreciation	380	
Gain on sale of investments	(50)	
Loss on sale of property, plant and equipment	45	
Investment income	(180)	
Interest costs	420	
	2,815	
Increase in trade receivables	(400)	
Increase in inventories	(390)	
Increase in payables	550	
Cash generated from operations	2,575	
Interest paid	(400)	
Income taxes paid	(760)	
Net cash from operating activities		1,415

242

	$'000	$'000
Cash flows from investing activities		
Acquisition of subsidiary (net of cash acquired)	(800)	
Acquisition of property, plant and equipment	(340)	
Proceeds from sale of equipment	70	
Proceeds from sale of investments	150	
Interest received	100	
Dividends received	80	
Net cash used in investing activities		(740)
Cash flows from financing activities		
Proceeds from share issue	300	
Proceeds from long term borrowings	300	
Dividend paid to owners of the parent	(1,000)	
Net cash used in financing activities		(400)
Net increase in cash and cash equivalents		275
Cash and cash equivalents at the beginning of the period		110
Cash and cash equivalents at the end of the period		385

Task

On 20th January 20X1, you receive the following email from Tim Grey:

From:	tg@fgh.co.uk
Sent:	20th January 20X1 11.30 a.m.
Subject:	Statement of cash flows

We need to prepare some information regarding FGH's statement of cash flows for the imminent board meeting.

The board's accounting knowledge is a bit rusty, so they will need some help understanding the three different categories of cash flows. More importantly, they will require an analysis of the statement of cash flow.

They have also identified a need to raise further finance for future expansion, both internally through investment in non-current assets, and externally through investments in local and overseas entities.

Please could you send me briefing notes in the form of an email which:

(1) Briefly explains how cash inflows and outflows should be classified and presented under the three headings of operating, investing and financing in a statement of cash flows prepared under the indirect method.

(2) Analyses the statement of cash flows of FGH, highlighting the key features of each category of cash flows.

(3) Briefly outlines which sources of finance would be the most appropriate to fund future purchase of non-current assets and investments.

Many thanks.

Kind regards

Tim Grey

Finance Director

Prepare the email requested by Tim Grey.

Task 35 Mocca

Indicative timing – 45 minutes (excluding Background Information)

Background information

Mocca Energy Group Limited ('Mocca') is an infrastructure and energy service company based in Algeria, specialised in the construction and operation of natural gas processing facilities in North Africa. Over the past decade, Mocca has built up a reputation as a respected player in the oil and gas industry, through a number of high-profile infrastructure projects carried out in partnership with large international energy companies. As well as constructing the infrastructure, Mocca also owns and operates two natural gas facilities, Shahrzad and Kalila.

The natural gas well Shahrzad – together with the right to extract natural gas from the well under a government licence – was acquired on 1 October 20X1 at a cost of $30 million. The terms of the licence are that Mocca will have to remove the well (which will then have no value) and restore the site to an environmentally satisfactory condition in 10 years' time when the natural gas reserves have been exhausted. The estimated cost decommissioning cost in 10 years' time will be $15 million.

On 15 November 20X1, Mocca acquired the Kalila natural gas well, together with the right to extract natural gas from the well under a government license. The license is valid for 10 years, but unlike the Shahrzad license, it does not state a legal obligation to restore the site at the end of the period.

On 1 April 20X1, Mocca entered into a three year construction contract with Poseidon to build a natural gas processing plant.

Mocca's weighted average cost of capital is 8%.

You are Selma Hayad, and you have worked as Financial Controller at Mocca for several years. You report to Saladin Maalouf, the Finance Director. Saladin Maalouf joined the company three months ago, replacing his predecessor with whom you had worked since you joined the company.

Mocca prepares its financial statements in accordance with IFRS. Its year end is 31 March.

Task

It is 5 April 20X2, and the Finance team is busy with year-end reporting. You receive the following email from the Finance Director:

From:	Saladin Maalouf smaalouf@mocca.com
Sent:	5th April 20X2, 2.15 p.m.
Subject:	Poseidon natural gas processing plant and well decommissioning

Hi Selma,

I hope you and your Finance colleagues are keeping your head above the water, this year end season!

As you know, I have been reviewing the financial reporting treatment of a number of significant transactions, not least because this helps me to get up to speed on the company's financial performance and position.

My knowledge of the financial reporting standards is a bit rusty, so I should like your opinion on two matters which have caught my attention:

- Recording of the construction contract for the Poseidon natural gas processing plant: A file note setting out the details of the construction contract and the current financial statement draft disclosures with workings are attached in **Exhibit 1**. The disclosures were prepared by a junior member of the finance team and I am not convinced they are correct.

- Accounting treatment of the decommissioning costs of two natural gas facilities: I believe you already have the details of our arrangements regarding the two gas facilities.

On a separate matter, we have recently launched a financing programme, as you know, to help ensure the company can grow sustainably in the mid- to long-term. It's important to avoid increasing Mocca's gearing, so we propose to issue 5 million 6% cumulative redeemable $1 preference shares in the second half of the year.

I will need to report to the board on the impact of each of these matters on our financial statements. Please prepare a briefing note in the form of an email, making reference to the applicable financial reporting standard where relevant, which:

(1)   identifies any adjustment required in respect of the Poseidon construction contract for the year ended 31 March 20X2, and explains why the current accounting treatment is incorrect;

(2)   explains in some detail the correct accounting treatment for the decommissioning costs arising from Shahrzad and Kalila in the financial statements for the year ended 31 March 20X2;

(3)   briefly explains how the preference shares would be classified in accordance with IAS 32 *Financial Instruments: Presentation* in the financial statements for the year ended 31 March 20X3, and the impact that this issue will have on the company's gearing.

There is no need to calculate the actual amount of any adjustment required.

Thank you in advance.

Kind regards,

Saladin Maalouf

Finance Director

Mocca Energy Group Limited

Draft the email as requested by Saladin.

Exhibit 1

File note: Details of Poseidon construction contract

	$'000
Total contract price	12,500
Costs incurred to date	4,000
Budgeted future costs	5,500
Progress billings invoiced	5,000
Progress billings received	4,900
Work certified to date	5,625

It is company policy to calculate the percentage of completion as the certified value of work completed as a percentage of the agreed contract price.

Draft financial statement disclosures

Profit or loss amounts

	$'000
Revenue	5,000
Cost of sales	(4,000)
Profit	1,000

Statement of financial position amounts

Current assets	$'000
Trade receivables (5,000 – 4,900)	100

Workings - total contract profit

	$'000
Contract price	12,500
Total expected costs	(9,500)
Total expected profit on contract	3,000

Task 36 Igbo

Indicative timing – 45 minutes (excluding Background Information)

Background information

On 1 June 20X5, Igbo, a public limited company incorporated in the country of Tigeria, was formed out of the reorganisation of a group of companies with foreign operations. The group structure is as follows:

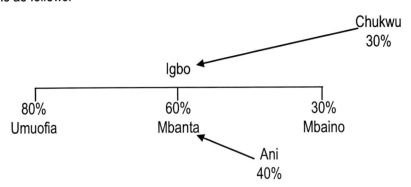

Under the group structure, Igbo owns 80% of Umuofia, 60% of Mbanta, and 30% of Mbaino. Igbo exercises significant influence over Mbaino.

The directors of Igbo are also directors of Umuofia and Mbaino.

The management board of Mbaino comprises five directors. Only one director of Igbo sits on the management board of Mbaino.

Originally the group comprised five companies but the fifth company, Ikeocha, which was a 70% subsidiary of Igbo, was sold on 31 January 20X6.

30% of the shares of Igbo are owned by another company, Chukwu, which exerts significant influence over Igbo. The remaining 40% of the shares of Mbanta are owned by Ani, which exerts significant influence over Mbanta.

Transactions with group companies and related parties

There were no transactions between Ikeocha and the Igbo Group during the year to 31 May 20X6.

During the current financial year to 31 May 20X6, Mbanta sold a significant amount of plant and equipment to Ani at the normal selling price for such items.

One of the directors of Umuofia, Marvellous Ikemefuna, who is not on the management board of Igbo, owns the whole of the share capital of a company, Elumelu.

Elumelu sells goods at market price to Umuofia.

Marvellous Ikemefuna is Production Director at Umuofia and also acts as a consultant to the management board of the group.

The currency in Tigeria is Tigerian dollars ('$' below).

You are Mark Okonkwo. Previously, you worked as Financial Controller for Umuofia, Igbo's foreign subsidiary in the country of Thedaria. Following the reorganisation, you were transferred on an expatriate contract to Igbo, where you are now the Group Financial Controller. You report to Lisa Ekwefi, the new Group Finance Director.

Task

It is now 20 June 20X6, and the group Finance team is busy finalising the group's financial statements for the year ended 31 May 20X6. You receive the following email from the Finance Director:

From:	lisaekwefi@igbo.com
Sent:	20th June, 9.30 a.m.
Subject:	Group reporting disclosures

Hi Mark,

I know it's all hands on deck for the year end group reporting right now, but I need you to spend a few minutes to look into a few financial reporting issues.

Firstly, I need your advice regarding how to account for our acquisition of Umuofia. As you know, Igbo purchased 80% of the ordinary share capital of Umuofia on 1 June 20X5 for 50 million Thedarian Crowns (TC) when its net assets were fair valued at 45 million TC. At 31 May 20X6, it is established that goodwill is impaired by 3 million TC. It is group policy to measure non-controlling interests at their proportionate share of the fair value of net assets.

I have just received a goodwill working from our external accountant, as part of the financial reporting pack related to the acquisition of Umuofia (**Exhibit 1**). I've only had a quick glance at it, but already it doesn't look quite right. I'd like you to review the workings to identify any errors. If there are any errors that are likely to have a pervasive impact on the rest of the financial reporting pack, I want to flag these up to the accountants so that they rectify the issues before we go any further.

Secondly, at the date of acquisition, Igbo made an interest free loan to Umuofia of $10 million. The loan is to be repaid on 31 May 20X7. An equivalent loan would normally carry an interest rate of 6% taking into account Umuofia's credit rating. The fair value of the interest-free loan, discounted to present value, is $8,900,000. An equivalent loan carrying a 6% interest has a discounted fair value of $9,434,000.

Financial liabilities of the group are normally measured at amortised cost. I need you to explain to me how the loan to Umuofia should be accounted for.

Lastly, the directors require your advice on the disclosure of related party information in the 20X6 group financial statements. I believe the International Financial Reporting Standards, which are adopted by the group, contain specific rules about the disclosure of related party transactions. However, Mr Unoka, our CEO, is reluctant to disclose too much information, as he feels that such transactions are a normal feature of business and need not be disclosed.

In order to conform with the IFRSs, I propose that where related party relationships are determined and sales are at normal selling price, any disclosures will state that prices charged to related parties are made on an arm's length basis.

Please prepare briefing notes in the form of an email for me which:

(1)   identifies the potential errors in the goodwill working for the Umuofia acquisition and explains, for each error, why the current treatment is incorrect and what the correct treatment should be;

(2)   explains how the loan to Umuofia should be treated in the financial statements of Umuofia for the year ended 31 May 20X6;

(3) sets out, in a format suitable for presentation to the board, notes on the financial reporting requirements around related party transactions. In particular, please

    (a) discuss why companies are required to disclose related party transactions

    (b) explain the criteria which determine a related party relationship.

    (c) describe the nature of any related party relationships and transactions which exists:

        – within the Igbo Group including Ikeocha
        – between Ani and the Igbo Group, and
        – between Chukwu and the Igbo Group

    and comment on whether each of the transactions mentioned in the group summary should be described as being at 'arm's length.'

Thanks in advance for your help.

Kind regards,

Lisa

Finance Director

Igbo Group

Please prepare the report as requested by Lisa.

Exhibit 1

Umuofia goodwill working

Goodwill is calculated and translated as follows:

	TC' m	Rate (Note)	$'m
Consideration transferred	50	2.3	21.7
Less fair value of identifiable net assets at acquisition	(45)	2.3	(19.6)
Goodwill at acquisition	5		2.1
Impairment	(3)	2.5	(1.2)
Irreconcilable difference	–		(0.1)
At 31 May 20X6	2	2.5	0.8

Note: The exchange rates were as follows:

	TC to $
1 June 20X5	2
31 May 20X6	2.5
Average rate for year	2.3

Topic 6 – F2 Further Tasks Solutions

Task 31

Marking scheme

	Marks	Marks
Sub-task 1		
Sale of land		
Identify that this is not a sale	2	
Explain IAS 18 criteria in the context of the scenario	5	
Explain correct accounting treatment	3	
Lease of Telecom Tower		
Identify that this is a finance lease	2	
Explain IAS 17 criteria in the context of the scenario	5	
Explain correct accounting treatment	3	
Other professional and ethical issues		
Identify ethical threat arising in FD's desire to maximise ROCE to attract investors	1	
Discussion of CIMA Code of Ethics: misleading information	3	
Discussion of CIMA Code of Ethics: professional competence and due care	2	
Available for sub-task 1	2̄6̄	
MAXIMUM FOR TASK		**25**

Suggested solution

REPORT

To: **Norman Koh**
Date: **10th February 20X4**
Subject: **Accounting treatment for the sale of land and the lease of the Telecom Tower**

<u>Introduction</u>

Thank you for your email. I set out explanations of each of the issues below.

<u>Sale of land</u>

We have treated the disposal of the land as a true sale by derecognising it from inventory and recording revenue in profit or loss.

This treatment follows the legal form of the transaction, but in reality, IAS 18's revenue recognition criteria have not been met. According to IAS 18, revenue should only be recognised for a sale of goods where all of the following criteria have been met:

(a) The entity has transferred to the buyer the significant risks and rewards of ownership of the goods;

(b) The entity retains neither continuing managerial involvement nor effective control over the goods sold;

(c) The amount of revenue can be measured reliably;

(d) It is probable that the economic benefits associated with the transaction will flow to the entity; and

(e)   Costs incurred in the transaction can be measured reliably.

In this case, Dragon Estates is keeping **the risks and rewards** associated with ownership of the land, as well as effective control. This is indicated by the following terms of the agreement:

- Veetle cannot use the land for any purpose without prior consent from Dragon Estates – this indicates that Dragon Estates is retaining effective control over the land.

- Although Dragon Estates only has the *option* to repurchase the land over the next four years, there is an *obligation* to repurchase it at the end of the fourth year if the option has not been exercised. This means that Dragon Estates retains the key risks (fall in value) and benefits (increase in value) of the land.

Therefore, the IAS 18 revenue recognition criteria have not been met and it would be incorrect to recognise revenue in respect of this transaction.

Instead, in substance, the sale of the land is a financing transaction rather a true sale. This is further supported by the following:

- The sale of the land is to a company that normally provides Dragon Estates with long-term finance; and

- The repurchase price increases over time, indicating an element of interest.

The sales proceeds should have been recorded as a loan rather than revenue.

The **adjustment required is to reinstate the land as inventory in Dragon Estates' statement of financial position at its cost of $1,310,000, reverse the revenue of $1,600,000, and record the sales proceeds as a liability.** The difference between the 31 December 20X4 repurchase price and the sales proceeds should be recorded as interest in the statement profit or loss for the year ended 31 December 20X4 and added to the carrying amount of the liability.

Telecom Tower lease

Leases are accounted for under IAS 17 *Leases*.

IAS 17 defines a finance lease as 'a lease that transfers substantially all the risks and rewards incidental to ownership of an asset' and gives five examples of situations that would normally lead to a lease being classified as a finance lease:

(a)   The present value of the minimum lease payments amounts to at least substantially all of the leased asset's fair value at inception:

(b)   The lease term is for the major part of the economic life of the asset even if title is not transferred to the lessee.

(c)   The lease transfers ownership of the asset to the lessee by the end of the lease term.

(d)   The lessee has the option to purchase the asset at a price sufficiently below fair value that it is reasonably certain at the inception of the lease that the lessee will exercise the option.

(e)   The leased assets are so specialised that only the lessee can use them without major modifications.

Although the building's useful life is unknown, the present value of the minimum lease payments ($1,890,000) exceeds the building's fair value at the inception of the lease ($1,880,000). Further, the contract states that the lease is non-cancellable and Dragon Estates retains the responsibility for maintaining the building as well as the liability for future damages. Even if we do not take up the option to purchase the building, these facts demonstrate clearly enough that Dragon Estates (the

lessee) has most of the risks and rewards associated with the asset and the lease should have been accounted for as a finance lease rather than an operating lease.

Therefore, **the operating lease rental expense of $10,500 for December 20X4 needs to be reversed**. Instead, **Telecom Tower should be recognised as an asset in the statement of financial position**, at $1,880,000, being the lower of its fair value ($1,880,000) and the present value of the minimum lease payments ($1,890,000). **A corresponding liability representing the obligation to pay the instalments on the lease until it expires should also be recognised**. Assets and liabilities cannot be netted off.

The building should then be depreciated over the shorter of its useful economic life and its lease term. A finance charge based on the implicit interest rate should also be expensed each year to the profit or loss account, as the finance lease liability unwinds. In the year ended 31 December 20X4, only one month of depreciation and finance charge need to be recorded as the inception of the lease was on 1 December 20X4.

If the accounting treatment for Telecom Tower is not corrected, then no asset would be recognised and lease payments would be expensed through the statement of profit or loss as they were incurred. This becomes 'off balance sheet finance'. We would then have assets in use and liabilities to lessors which are not recorded in the financial statements. This would be misleading to the users of the accounts and make it appear as though the assets which were recorded were more efficient in producing returns than was actually the case.

Other professional and ethical issues

While it is important to secure investment, it is unethical to make our financial statements more attractive to investors by deviating from the IFRSs.

We are both CIMA-qualified management accountants, and therefore we are bound to act in accordance with CIMA's *Code of Ethics*.

The *Code of Ethics* clearly states that members should not be associated with reports, returns, communications or other information where they believe that the information contains a materially false or misleading statement.

Accounting for the sale of land as revenue would cause the company's profit to be overstated, and its liabilities to be understated. Accounting for the lease of Telecom Tower as an operating lease would cause the company's assets and liabilities to be understated. If the accounting treatment is not corrected, this will have an impact on key ratios. Gearing would be understated due to the missing liabilities from the sale of the land and the finance lease. This would be misleading as it would make Dragon Estates' appear less risky than it really is. Return on capital employed would be overstated due to the profit incorrectly recognised on the sale of the land and the capital employed being understated by the missing liabilities in relation to the sale of land and the finance lease. As a result, this would convey a misleading picture of Dragon Estates being more capable of generating high returns from its assets than it really is.

At the same time, by not complying with the IAS 18 *Revenue* and IAS 17 *Leases* and the principles of the *Conceptual Framework*, we would also fail to exercise **professional competence and due care**, one of the *Code*'s fundamental principles.

Conclusion

I hope the above explanations of the accounting treatment are clear. Please do get in contact if you have any queries.

Competency coverage

Sub-task	Technical		Business acumen		People		Leadership		Max
1	Apply IAS 18 and 19 to explain the correct accounting treatment for the land disposal and lease. Demonstrate knowledge of the Code of Ethics in assessing the ethical issues arising.	25							25
Total		25							25

Task 32

Marking scheme

	Marks	Marks
Sub-task 1		
Explanation of accounting treatment (1 mark per valid point)		
Denzyl – subsidiary	6	
Formalight - associate	3	
Ullenvitte – subsidiary (partial disposal)	4	
Blueskye – subsidiary (step acquisition)	4	
Maximum for sub-task 1		17
Sub-task 2		
Individual financial statements: Explanation of how to determine functional currency		5
Sub-task 3		
Consolidated financial statements: Explanation of how to translate to reporting currency		3
MAXIMUM FOR TASK		25

Suggested solution

EMAIL

Accounting treatment for investments

Investment in Denzyl

Century has acquired 90% of the issued ordinary share capital of Denzyl. Therefore, it has **control** of Denzyl, which should be **fully consolidated as a subsidiary** under the provisions of IFRS 10 *Consolidated financial statements*. As the subsidiary was acquired mid-year, the income, expenses and other comprehensive income of Denzyl should be pro-rated in the consolidated statement of profit or loss and other comprehensive income for the six months that Century had control.

In the consolidated statement of financial position, Denzyl should be consolidated with a 10% non-controlling interest.

Based on the workings that you provided, we acquired Denzyl with negative goodwill of $120,000. This is treated as a **bargain purchase** and the $120,000 will be **credited to profit or loss in the year of acquisition.**

In addition, the fair value uplift of $1m relates to property. This will result in **additional depreciation of $25,000 each year** ($1m/40). The depreciation should be time apportioned so in 20X8 only $12,500 (6/12 × $25,000) will be charged.

Investment in Formalight

Century has acquired 40% of the issued ordinary share capital of Formalight. Therefore, it can be presumed to exercise **significant influence** over Formalight, which should be treated **as an associate** under the provisions of IAS 28 (Revised) *Investments in associates and joint ventures*. Formalight will be included in the group financial statements using **equity accounting**. In the consolidated statement of financial position, the investment should be measured at cost on initial recognition and then in each subsequent period the group share of Formalight's post acquisition retained reserves should be added on and any impairment deducted. In the consolidated statement of profit or loss and other comprehensive income, the group share (40%) of Formalight's profit and other comprehensive income should be included.

Investment in Ullenvitte

Before the disposal on 1 October 20X7, we had control of Ullenvitte with an 80% shareholding, making Ullenvitte a subsidiary. On 1 October 20X7, the group sold 20,000 of Ullenvitte's 250,000 shares - an 8% shareholding, leaving us with a 72% shareholding. The group therefore still retains control of Ullenvitte. After the disposal, Ullenvitte is still a subsidiary – the disposal is simply a decrease in the controlling interest in Ullenvitte.

In substance, therefore, no disposal has taken place. This is simply a **transaction between group shareholders:** the group has sold 8% shares to the non-controlling interest. Non-controlling interest will increase by 8% and there will also be an adjustment to the Century group's equity (ie retained earnings).

In the consolidated statement of profit or loss and other comprehensive income, Ullenvitte will be consolidated for the full year as Ullenvitte was a subsidiary for the full year. However, non-controlling interest will need to be pro-rated: 20% for the first nine months of the year and 28% for the last three months of the year.

In the consolidated statement of financial position, Ullenvitte will be consolidated as it is still a subsidiary at the year end, with a corresponding non-controlling interest of 28% based on the year end shareholding.

Investment in Blueskye

After the second acquisition on 1 October 20X7, Century holds a total of 55% of the issued ordinary share capital of Blueskye and so has control of Blueskye from that date.

Before 1 October 20X7, Century did not exercise either control or significant influence over Blueskye. The holding should be treated as an available for sale financial asset up to 30 September 20X7, measuring the investment at fair value with any gains or losses recognised in other comprehensive income.

Then the investment will be treated as a subsidiary from 1 October 20X7 under the provisions of IFRS 10 *Consolidated financial statements*. This means that Blueskye should be consolidated from 1 October 20X7 in the group statement of profit or loss and other comprehensive income for the year ended 31 December 20X7, by pro-rating for three months' control. As Blueskye is a subsidiary at 31 December 20X7, full consolidation will also be required in the consolidated statement of financial position.

In a step acquisition where control is achieved, IFRS 3 *Business combinations* requires a gain or loss on the original investment to be recognised in profit or loss. The gain is calculated as the fair value at the date control is achieved (1 October 20X7) less the original cost of the investment, giving a gain of $700,000 ($1.7m - $1m).

The fair value of this 15% investment at the date control is achieved is then used in the goodwill calculation alongside the consideration paid for the 40% investment ($4.5 million). In substance, on 1 October 20X7, Century has purchased a 55% investment, which is why goodwill must be calculated on the full 55% shareholding. Non-controlling interest will be calculated at 1 October 20X7 as 45% of Blueskye's net assets at that date.

Functional currency of Hermosa

IAS 21 *The effects of changes in foreign exchange rates* defines the **functional currency** as the **currency of the primary economic environment in which the entity operates**. This is the currency used to measure the results and financial position of the entity.

IAS 21 lists **factors to consider** in determining the functional currency of an entity. The following factors indicate that should Hermosa be moved overseas, the functional currency of Hermosa would become the Guatemalan Quetzal:

(a)   The country whose competitive forces and regulations **mainly determine the sales prices of goods or services**. As Hermosa would be subject to local corporate regulations, this indicates the functional currency would be the GTQ.

(b)   The currency that **mainly influences labour, material and other costs**. Hermosa would source all material locally, recruit a local workforce and be subject to local taxes.

(c)   Whether the activities of the foreign operation are carried out as an **extension of the reporting entity or with a degree of autonomy.** Hermosa has operated relatively autonomously since acquisition and this is expected to continue.

(d)   Whether **transactions with the reporting entity are a high or low proportion of the foreign operation's activities**. In the year ended 31 December 20X9, Hermosa sold $200,000 of goods to the group, representing 6% of Hermosa's total revenue. This is a relatively low level of intra-group trading.

(e)   The currency that **mainly influences sales price for goods and services**. 85% of Hermosa's total revenue come from the Central and South American market. As it is unclear what portion of these sales would be to Guatemala and in GTQ, no one currency presents itself as the currency mainly influencing the sales price.

Even though the last factor is inconclusive, the majority of the factors indicate that after the move, the functional currency of Hermosa would be the GTQ. Therefore, from the move, Hermosa should maintain its nominal ledger and prepare its financial statements in GTQ.

Translation of Hermosa

For consolidation purposes, IAS 21 *The effects of changes in foreign exchange rates* requires that the financial statements of Hermosa be translated using the presentation currency of the group accounts (the Schwarz $). The statement of financial position assets and liabilities are translated at the spot rate of exchange on the reporting date (ie 31 December 20X9) and the statement of profit or loss is translated at the spot rate on the date of each transaction, or at a weighted average rate of exchange for the year. Any exchange differences are not reported in profit or loss, as they have no impact on the cash flows of the group, but instead are reported as other comprehensive income (items that may subsequently be reclassified to profit or loss) and a separate translation reserve.

Competency coverage

Sub-task	Technical		Business acumen		People		Leadership		Max
1	Explaining the accounting treatment of investments	17							17
2	Currency translation issues: identify the functional currency	5							5
3	Currency translation issues: explain how foreign subsidiary's results should be translated	3							3
Total		25							25

Task 33

Marking scheme

	Marks	Marks
Sub-task 1		
Explanation and evaluation of investors' ratios		
For each ratio, maximum of 3 marks		6
Sub-task 2		
Analysis of Fermion's financial performance:		
2 marks for each relevant and well-explained point		
(on ratios & financial statements)	8	
Analysis of Fermion's financial position:		
2 marks for each relevant and well-explained point		
(on ratios & financial statements)	8	
Relevant conclusion (can be presented after Sub-task 3)	2	
Available for sub-task 2	18	
Maximum for sub-task 2		**16**
Sub-task 3		
Identification of useful post-year end information:		
1 mark for each relevant type of information where reason given		3
MAXIMUM FOR TASK		25

Suggested solution

1. **REPORT**

   To: Rachel Higgs
   Date: 20th May 20X2
   Subject: Re: Investment plans

   Hi Rachel,

   Thank you for your email.

   <u>Introduction</u>

   This report will:

   (i)   Explain below the basis on which dividend yield and asset turnover ratios are calculated, and the suitability of each ratio for the initial and on-going appraisal and comparison of potential investment targets.

   (ii) Analyse the financial performance and financial position of Fermion and make a recommendation as to Fermion's suitability for investment based upon the information available.

   (iii) Discuss what post year-end information might be available that would provide us with additional information before we make an investment decision.

<u>Suitable investors' ratios</u>

Dividend yield

Dividend yield is the ratio of the dividend to the market value of a share. The dividend yield is the cash component of the total return of an investment.

Usually, only a small proportion of the total return from equity investments is attributable to dividends, the bulk being attributed to the capital gain from the investment. For this reason, the dividend yield is not normally a good indication of the potential return from an equity investment.

A high dividend yield may be an indication that a company lacks investment opportunities, preferring to return cash to its shareholders in the form of dividends rather than investing in new projects and returning value to its shareholders in the form of higher share prices. In some countries where the tax system is more favourable to capital gains than to dividends, a low dividend yield may simply indicate, not the financial strength of a company, but an optimal response to the tax treatment. Finally, dividend payments are sometimes perceived as signalling the financial robustness of a company (the so called **signalling effect**) and must be paid even if paying them leads to the abandonment of profitable investment opportunities.

Dividend yield is of more interest to an income-seeking investor rather than a capital-growth seeking investor. Given that Boson is looking to expand, capital growth and the amount of profit reinvested in the business are likely to be of more interest than the dividend paid out. Therefore, unless Boson has a specific need to raise cash, it would also be of limited use as an ongoing appraisal tool.

Asset turnover ratios

There is a variety of asset turnover ratios, all of which are calculated by dividing revenue by the value of specific assets owned by the company. These ratios measure the efficiency of asset use since they compare the amount of revenues generated per unit of assets owned by the company. The ratio can be defined in terms of the total assets of a company or in terms of sub-categories, for example, non-current and current assets.

The ratio can be used as an investment criterion. Investors would prefer a target with a high asset turnover ratio to one with a low one. However, comparability between entities can be distorted by factors such as different accounting policies (e.g. revaluation, depreciation policies), different ages of assets and different methods of acquiring assets (e.g. cash versus operating lease).

The revenues can also be affected by revenue recognition policies that individual entities may have in place.

The ratio is of greater use as an ongoing appraisal tool for an individual entity.

<u>Analysis of Fermion's financial performance and position</u>

Financial performance

Fermion has expanded during the year with a growth in revenue of 9.7%. This is a good achievement given the highly competitive market that Fermion operates in and the new entrant to the market offering a lower sales price.

However, this expansion appears to be at the cost of profitability. The profit for the year has fallen by 35%.

This is partly due to the gross margin declining from 35% in 20X1 to 32.4% in 20X2. This is probably as a result of lowering the sales price in order to compete with the new entrant to the market.

On a more positive note, Fermion appears to be controlling its overheads well, with operating expenses falling slightly and an improvement in operating margin (despite the fall in gross margin) from 4.9% to 5.2%.

This operating margin was calculated without taking into account the associate. The associate has had a detrimental effect on net profit margin in the current year as it made a loss in 20X2 compared to a profit in 20X1. The poor performance of the associate and the cash flow difficulties that Fermion is experiencing (see below) suggests it may be preferable to sell the associate.

Net profit has also suffered from a 138% increase in finance costs. This is largely due to a positive cash balance of $24m in 20X1 deteriorating into an overdraft of $47m in 20X2.

The fall in share price in 20X2 reflects the general downturn in the stock market but also the decline in results compared to 20X1 although the final dividend did boost the share price to some extent.

Investors will have been disappointed by the fall in EPS from 70c in 20X1 to 40c in 20X2 but the dividend will have compensated for this fall to some extent. The fact that the P/E ratio has increased from 6.20 in 20X1 to 6.25 in 20X2 indicates that the market has confidence in the future success of Fermion despite the decline in profitability.

Financial position

Fermion is suffering from considerable liquidity problems in 20X2. The quick ratio has deteriorated from 1.06 to 0.49 meaning that the company may struggle to pay its current liabilities out of receivables and cash.

Fermion is reliant on a significant overdraft of $47m. This is very close to the limit on the facility of $50m. An overdraft is a risky source of finance as it could be withdrawn at any point by the bank. Furthermore, short term borrowings usually attract a higher rate of interest than long term borrowings making them more expensive. Fermion's cash flow problems are largely due to poor working capital management. Inventory days have increased from 100 days to 167 days resulting in significant holding costs for the company and the risk of obsolescence. This is an indication that Fermion is struggling to sell its inventory as a result of the competition from the new entrant in the market. Given that Fermion is a technology company, which is a dynamic, fast-moving sector, the risk of inventory obsolescence is high.

Receivable days have also increased from 61 days to 64 days, indicating that Fermion could improve its credit control function in order to collect debts from customers more quickly.

Payable days have increased significantly from 109 days to 156 days. This is an indication that Fermion are struggling to pay their suppliers. Whilst it is advisable to take advantage of the free credit provided by the suppliers, exceeding the credit terms to such an extent is highly risky. There is a danger that Fermion's suppliers might withdraw their credit or stop supplying altogether.

During the year, Fermion has revalued its property, plant and equipment. Given that long term borrowings are only $90m compared to property, plant and equipment of $393m, there are significant assets still available as potential security for future debt finance.

Fermion has also purchased a significant amount of new assets in the year. Presumably, this was to help the increased production required for the expansion in the year. The extra depreciation resulting from the revaluation and asset purchase could be part of the reason for the fall in gross margin.

Post year end information

It would be useful to know:

(i)   The post-year end share price of Fermion to see if the share price has been maintained at its increased level of $2.50 resulting from the dividend announcement or whether it has fallen in light of the year end financial statements.

(ii)   The share price, EPS and P/E ratio of the new entrant to the market for comparison purposes as well as industry averages.

(iii)   Details of any inventory write down post year end given the high level of inventory at the year end.

(iv)   Post year end sales to see if the large amount of inventory held at year end has been sold off.

(v)   Details of any correspondence with the bank to see if the short-term borrowing facility is to be maintained or even increased.

Conclusion

Fermion is worth considering for investment as it is growing despite the new competitor in the market and is still profitable and is controlling its overheads well. It also has a higher quality product than the new entrant. The P/E ratio has increased despite the decline in profitability indicating the market's confidence in the future of Fermion.

However, significant improvement is required to its working capital management, and refinancing will be necessary in the near future as it is reaching its overdraft limit and will need to repay its long term borrowings in three years' time. Furthermore, there is a need to improve Fermion's gross margin with efficiencies in its production costs to compensate for the fall in sales price required to compete with the new entrant to the market.

We will need to consider carefully whether Boson is ready to invest the time and resources required to implement improvements to Fermion's working capital practices. The Board will also need to consider the extent to which synergies between Boson and Fermion's businesses will allow efficiencies to be achieved.

Competency coverage

Sub-task	Technical		Business acumen		People		Leadership		Max
1	Explain investors' ratios	6							6
2	Perform financial analysis and make recommendations	16							16
3	Identify missing information	3							3
Total		25							25

Task 34

Marking scheme

	Marks	Marks

Sub-task 1 – Explanation of headings in the statement of cash flows

Operating
- Day to day activities — 1
- Adjustments for non-cash items & items to be reported under a different heading — 1

Investing
- Buying and selling non-current assets — 1
- Including intangible, tangible & investments — 1

Financing
- Issuing and repaying long term finance (debt & equity) — 1
- Often includes dividends paid (but can be presented as 'operating' instead) — <u>1</u>

Maximum for sub-task 1 — <u>6</u>

Sub-task 2 – Analysis of FGH's statement of cash flows

Operating
- Profitable & healthy inflows from main operations — 1
- Significant portion of cash from operations used to pay tax & interest — 1
- Interest payments will increase in future due to new borrowings — 1
- Increase in receivables, inventories & payables likely to be due to expansion — 1

Investing
- Acquired new subsidiary in the year ($800,000) – part of expansion — 1
- Purchased new PPE in the year ($340,000) – part of expansion — 1
- Resulted in net outflow but should lead to increased profits and cash flows from operations in future years — 1
- Equipment sold at a loss – implies FGH purchased new PPE to replace old & inefficient assets — 1
- Sale of investments at a gain imply that they were generating a strong return which will not recur in the future — 1
- Proceeds from sale of investments partly used to finance the acquisition of the subsidiary, the purchase of PPE and the expansion — 1

Financing
- Raised $600,000 new finance to help fund the acquisition and expansion — 1
- Equal amounts of debt and equity – minimal impact on gearing — 1
- Dividend payment of $1 million = high payout (71% of cash from operating activities) – if had not been paid, would not have needed to raise new finance — <u>1</u>

Maximum for sub-task 2 — <u>13</u>

	Marks	Marks
Sub-task 3 – Sources of finance		
Term of finance (fund long-term assets with long-term finance = matching)	1	
Equity (listed so can issue shares to public, irredeemable so no repayment required, dividends at discretion of directors)	2	
Debt (bank borrowings but have existing borrowings so security could be an issue, loan covenants, bonds/loan notes, cheaper than equity)	2	
Other (1 mark per point): leases, foreign exchange, convertible debt	3	
Available for sub-task 3	$\overline{8}$	
Maximum for sub-task 3		6
MAXIMUM FOR TASK		$\overline{\underline{25}}$

Suggested solution

BRIEFING NOTES

<u>Headings in the statement of cash flows</u>

Operating activities

This section reports the cash inflows and outflows resulting from the day to day activities of FGH – buying raw materials, paying salaries and overheads, selling finished goods and so on.

FGH's statement of cash flows has been prepared under the indirect method. This means that the starting point of the statement of cash flows is profit before tax then adjustments are made to:

- remove non-cash items (e.g. depreciation)

- remove items that should live elsewhere in the cash flow (e.g. investment income)

- record the movement in working capital (increase/decrease in inventories, receivables and payables).

Below the sub-total of cash generated from operations, the indirect costs of operations (interest and tax paid) are shown.

It is operating cash flows which must, in the end, pay for cash outflows relating to other activities, such as purchasing non-current assets and paying dividends. Otherwise, new finance will have to be raised to fund these outflows.

Investing activities

This section includes cash inflows and outflows from buying and selling tangible non-current assets, intangible non-current assets and investments. The cash return on these investments including dividends and interest received is also included here.

The cash flows under this heading show the extent of new investment in assets which will generate future profit and cash flows.

Financing activities

Cash inflows and outflows from issuing and repaying long-term finance (both debt and equity) are included here. Dividends paid are often included here too, although they may also be shown in 'operating activities'.

The financing cash flows indicate the likely future claims on the company's finance from providers of capital.

Analysis of statement of cash flows

Cash from operating activities

The operating activities section of FGH's statement of cash flows shows that the business is not only profitable, but is generating healthy inflows of cash from its main operations.

A significant proportion of the cash generated from operations is utilised in paying tax and interest on borrowings. The amount needed to pay interest in future may increase as the company appears to be increasing its borrowings to fund its expansion.

The adjustments to profit show that receivables, inventories and payables are all increasing. This trend may reflect the expansion of the business but working capital management must be reviewed carefully to ensure that cash is collected promptly from receivables so that we are able to meet our obligations to pay our suppliers and maintain good trading relationships.

Cash from investing activities

The two main investing outflows in the year were the net cash payment of $800,000 to acquire a new subsidiary and the payment of $340,000 to acquire new property, plant and equipment. These are a clear reflection of the strategy of expansion and may lead to increased profits and cash flows from operations in future years.

This section also reflects cash received from the sale of equipment of $70,000 and the operating cash flows section shows that this equipment was sold at a loss. This suggests that FGH acquired the new equipment to replace assets that were old and inefficient.

The most significant inflow in this section is an amount of $150,000 from the sale of investments, probably to help finance the acquisition and expansion. The fact that these investments were sold at a gain of $50,000 indicates that these investments were generating a strong return. This type of cash flow is unlikely to recur in future and also means that the other inflows in this section, the interest and dividends received, are likely to cease or be reduced in future.

Cash from financing activities

The company has raised new finance totalling $600,000, which has probably been applied to the acquisition and expansion. The new finance comprises equal amounts of equity and borrowings perhaps with the deliberate intention of minimising the impact on gearing. The increased borrowings will mean that future interest expenses will increase, which could threaten profitability in future if the expansion does not create an immediate increase in operating profits.

This section also includes the largest single cash flow, a dividend payment of $1,000,000. This is a high proportion of cash generated from operating activities (71%). If this dividend had not been paid, FGH would not have needed to raise new finance to fund the expansion. Presumably, it indicates FGH's directors' confidence that the expanded business will generate returns that will easily cover the additional interest costs, and allow this level of dividend payment to continue in future.

Conclusion

The expansion appears to have been very successful both in terms of profitability and cash flow. We must be careful not to pay excessive dividends in the future at the cost of reinvesting in the business.

Sources of finance

Term of finance

The term of the finance should be matched with the life of the asset it is used to purchase.

Investments and non-current assets for the purpose of expansion are likely to be held for the long term. Therefore, it makes sense to finance these purchases with long term sources of finance. A short-term source of finance like an overdraft would not be appropriate – it would be more expensive as short-term finance attracts a higher rate of interest and more risky as it could be recalled.

Debt and equity

The two main types of long-term finance available are debt or equity. As FGH is a listed entity, we could raise finance by issuing shares to the public.

The key advantage of debt over equity is that it tends to cheaper, as interest is typically a tax allowable expense. It also avoids the dilution of the company's earnings per share, which would occur if equity finance is used.

However, equity is typically irredeemable so no repayment would be required and the payment of dividends is at the discretion of the directors. It also ensures that our level of gearing, which may be regarded by investors as an indicator of risk, does not increase.

Debt options include bank borrowings, but as we have existing borrowings, we would need to make sure that there were sufficient assets available to offer the bank as security. We would also need to make sure that we do not enter into any unacceptable loan covenants which would restrict our business activities. Other debt options would include a bond or loan note issue. These might be more attractive to potential lenders as they would be able to sell them on.

Convertible debt is another possibility as we could benefit from a lower rate of interest, in return for offering a right to a share at the redemption date. However, we would need to carefully consider the impact on our investor ratios when the debt is converted into shares.

Leases

An alternative to purchasing new assets outright would be to enter into a lease thereby avoiding the need for a large initial cash outflow. There are two types of lease – an operating lease (where the asset is typically leased for a small part of its useful life) and a finance lease (where the asset is typically leased for most of its useful life). Finance leases would be a more appropriate long term source of finance but would have an adverse effect on gearing as a lease liability would be recorded in the statement of financial position. Operating leases are not recorded in the statement of financial position – instead a rental expense is recognised in profit or loss.

Foreign exchange

If the investment is in an overseas entity and has to be paid for in a foreign currency, it would be a good idea to raise finance in the same foreign currency. This would protect us against adverse movements in exchange rates as if there is an exchange loss on the investment, an exchange gain would arise on the loan and vice versa.

Competency coverage

Sub-task	Technical		Business acumen		People		Leadership		Max
1	Headings in cash flow	6							6
2	Identification of key inflows and outflows and performing financial analysis based on cash flows	13							13
3	Explanation of different sources of finance	6							6
Total		25							25

Task 35

Marking scheme

	Marks	Marks
Sub-task 1		
Construction contract – 2 marks per valid well-explained point		
Identification as construction contract and explanation of		
IAS 11 accounting treatment	2	
Explanation of how stage of completion is calculated	2	
Identification of error and explanation of impact on P/L and SOFP	4	
Maximum for sub-task 1		**8**
Sub-task 2		
Decommissioning costs – 2 marks per valid well-explained point		
Shahrzad – Non-current asset	2	
Shahrzad – Provision	2	
Shahrzad – Finance cost/ Depreciation	2	
Kalila – No provision if no constructive obligation	2	
Kalila – What may cause constructive obligation	2	
Kalila – Subsequent treatment if constructive obligation exists	2	
Maximum for sub-task 2		**12**
Sub-task 3		
Classification as financial liability and explanation why	3	
Treat dividends as finance cost	1	
Impact on gearing	1	
Maximum for sub-task 3		**5**
MAXIMUM FOR TASK		**25**

Suggested solution

BRIEFING NOTES

Poseidon construction contract

The construction of the Poseidon natural gas plant, which straddles three accounting periods, should be accounted for as a construction contract under IAS 11 *Construction contracts*.

Where the outcome of a contract can be estimated reliably, as here, the contract revenue and costs should be recognised according to the stage of completion of the contract. In each accounting period, the revenue, costs and profit arising from the contract are attributed to the proportion of work completed at the end of that accounting period.

IAS 11 allows a choice of three methods for determining the stage of completion of construction contracts: proportion of contract costs incurred, surveys of work performed, and physical proportion completed. The surveys of work performed approach which calculates the stage of completion as a percentage of work certified to be completed over the total contract price is the method that we adopt.

271

The stage of completion that should have been used for the financial statements disclosures is:

$$\text{Work completed} = \frac{\text{Work certified}}{\text{Contract price}} = \frac{\$5,625,000}{\$12,500,000} = 45\%$$

The draft disclosures are incorrect because revenue had been stated at amounts invoiced to the customer ($5m) and cost of sales has been stated at amounts incurred to date ($4m).

The amounts should have been calculated based on the total contract price ($12,500,000) multiplied by 45% stage of completion above.

Cost of sales should be calculated as 45% of the total expected costs (costs to date of $4m + budgeted costs to completion of $5.5m).

Correcting this error would result in recognising 45% of the total contract profit (total contract price less total expected costs) instead of the $1,000,000 as currently stated.

The trade receivables balance of $100,000 in the statement of financial position disclosure has been calculated correctly as amounts invoiced less amounts received from customers. However, an additional amount needs to be disclosed in the statement of financial position under 'current assets' with the heading 'gross amounts due from customers'. This should be calculated as costs incurred to date ($4m) plus recognised profit to date less progress billings to date ($5m).

[Tutorial note: No marks will be awarded for calculating the correct P/L and SOFP disclosures, or quantifying the adjustments, but they will be awarded for explaining how to calculate the figures correctly.]

Decommissioning costs

Shahrzad

A provision should be recognised in respect of the decommissioning costs, in accordance with IAS 37 *Provisions, contingent liabilities and contingent assets*.

Mocca must provide for dismantling and restoration costs at 31 March 20X2. This is because IAS 37's three criteria for a provision have been met:

- There is a legal obligation under the licensing agreement and an obligating event took place with the purchase of the well prior to the year end on 1 October 20X1;
- There is a probable outflow under the terms of the licence, Mocca will have to pay to remove the well in 10 years' time;
- There is a reliable estimate of the cost in 10 years' time ($15m).

The amount of the provision will be the present value of the future cash flow of $15m discounted at the weighted average cost of capital of 8%. The discount will be 'unwound' each year and debited to finance costs. The credit entry will increase the provision until it stands at $15m at the end of 10 years.

The other side of the double entry for the provision is to add the present value of the decommissioning costs to the carrying amount of the asset. This should then be depreciated over 10 years.

Kalila

As the licence does not require an environmental clean-up, Mocca has no legal obligation to restore the site at the end of the licence.

It is then necessary to determine whether or not we have a constructive obligation. This would apply if Mocca has a published policy of removing wells and restoring the site at the end of the licence, or

the company has established an expectation that it will carry out an environmental clean-up where required. If either of these were the case, then a constructive obligation would exist and a provision would be required.

Cumulative redeemable preference shares

IAS 32 requires that financial instruments are classified according to their substance, rather than their legal form.

The main distinguishing feature of a liability is that it contains an obligation to transfer economic benefit.

In this case the preference shares are redeemable so the company has an obligation to pay back the capital to the shareholders. Furthermore, they are cumulative which means that we have an obligation to pay the 6% dividend – even if there were insufficient distributable reserves to pay it in any one year, it would become payable in the future when sufficient distributable reserves arise.

Therefore, these preference shares should be classified as liabilities and this will increase Mocca's gearing.

The treatment of dividends should be consistent with the treatment of the instrument. Therefore dividends should be classified as a finance cost in profit or loss rather than an appropriation of profit in the statement of changes in equity.

Competency coverage

Sub-task	Technical	Business acumen		People		Leadership		Max
1	Explain correct accounting treatment of construction contract and describe the adjustments required	8						8
2	Explain the accounting treatment with respect to the decommissioning costs	12						12
3	Identification of correct accounting treatment for preference shares and describe the impact on gearing	5						5
Total		25						25

Task 36

Marking scheme

	Marks	Marks
Sub-task 1		
Identification and explanation of errors in Umuofia goodwill working		
Exchange rate used	2	
Non-controlling interest	4	
Exchange difference	2	
Maximum for sub-task 1		**8**
Sub-task 2		
Explanation of loan treatment – 2 marks per relevant well-explained point		6
Sub-task 3		
Reason for disclosing related party transactions	3	
Explanation of related party criteria:		
• Persons	1	
• Entities	2	
Nature of related party relationships and transactions:		
Igbo	5	
Ani	3	
Chukwu	3	
Total available for sub-task 3	17	
Maximum for sub-task 3		**11**
MAXIMUM FOR TASK		**25**

Suggested solution

BRIEFING NOTES

<u>Goodwill arising on the acquisition of Umuofia</u>

The current workings contain three errors:

(1)   Exchange rate

IAS 21 *The effect of changes in foreign exchange rates* states that goodwill arising on the acquisition of a foreign subsidiary should be expressed in the functional currency of the foreign operation and retranslated at the closing rate at each year-end. This has been done correctly.

The goodwill at acquisition, however, should not be calculated based on the average rate during year (2.3), but should be based on the spot rate at the date of acquisition (2). Given the large amounts involved, this translation error is likely to give rise to a material impact not only on the value of goodwill, but also on the value of net assets recognised in the group financial statements.

(2)   Non-controlling interests

Only 80% of Umuofia's ordinary shares have been acquired by the group. The remaining 20% are held by non-controlling interests.

Non-controlling interests, valued at its proportionate share of the fair value of the net assets, should have been added to the value of consideration transferred in calculating the goodwill at acquisition.

Based on a fair value of identifiable net assets of TC 45 million, I would expect to see non-controlling interest of TC 9 million (45 million at 20%) to be included in the workings. This would then be translated at the spot rate at the date of acquisition (2) to give us a non-controlling interest value of $4.5 million.

As a result of the omission of non-controlling interests, the goodwill at acquisition would have been understated by $4.5 million. More worryingly, it is possible that this error indicates that non-controlling interests have been overlooked elsewhere. If this is the case, not only goodwill but retained earnings will be misstated, and disclosures in both the consolidated statement of profit or loss and other comprehensive income and the consolidated statement of financial position would be incorrect if non-controlling interest is not disclosed.

(3)   Exchange difference

The irreconcilable difference (the balancing figure between the translated goodwill at acquisition after impairment, and the translated goodwill balance at the year end) is in fact the exchange difference. At the moment, it is incorrectly showing as a small gain due to the two errors above, which has caused goodwill on acquisition to be overstated. An exchange loss will arise, after the working is corrected for the two previous errors.

The exchange loss should be recalculated and **recognised in other comprehensive income (items that may subsequently be reclassified to profit or loss)**, and taken to the translation reserve in equity.

The fact that the exchange loss is identified as an irreconcilable difference suggests that it has not been recorded in other comprehensive income and equity.

Tutorial note:

Calculations are not required. However, for your reference, the correct goodwill working, after adjusting for the above errors are as follows:

	TC'm	Rate	$m
Consideration transferred	50		25.0
Non-controlling interests (45 × 20%)	9	2	4.5
Less: fair value of net assets at acquisition	(45)		(22.5)
Goodwill at acquisition	14		7.0
Impairment	(3)	2.5	(1.2)
Exchange loss (balancing figure)			(1.4)
At 31 May 20X6	11	2.5	4.4

Loan to Umuofia

From Umuofia's perspective, as the borrower, the loan is a **financial liability.** The loan is measured at **fair value** on initial recognition and subsequently at **amortised cost** because it is not 'held for trading'.

Fair value is defined as the price that would be received to sell an asset or paid to transfer a liability in an orderly transaction between market participants at the measurement date. This would normally be the actual transaction price. However, Igbo and Umuofia are related parties and the transaction **has not taken place on normal commercial terms**.

IAS 39 states that it is necessary to **establish what the transaction price would have been** in an orderly transaction between market participants at the measurement date. In this case, the fair value of the interest-bearing loan is a more reliable indication of what the transaction price would have been, based on normal commercial terms. Therefore $9,434,000 should be taken to be the fair value of the loan, which should then be **retranslated at the closing rate** at the year-end. This should be the value at which the loan is recognised in Umuofia's financial statements.

The **unwinding of the discount** is recognised as a **finance cost** in profit or loss for the year, at the average rate for the year. The **exchange loss** is also **recognised in profit or loss**.

Related party transactions

Reason for related party disclosure requirements

You are correct in saying that related party transactions are a normal feature of business. However, by their nature, the related party transactions can affect the **financial performance and position** of the companies on both sides of the transaction.

An obvious instance of this is where one group company sells goods to another at artificially low prices. Even where there are no actual transactions between group companies, **a parent normally influences the way in which a subsidiary operates**.

In the absence of other information, users of the financial statements **assume that a company pursues its interests independently** and undertakes transactions on an **arm's length basis** on terms that could have been obtained in a transaction with a third party.

Knowledge of related party relationships and transactions affects the way in which users assess a company's operations and the risks and opportunities that it faces. Therefore, **details of an entity's controlling party and transactions with related parties should be disclosed**. Even if the company's transactions and operations have not been affected by a related party relationship, **disclosure makes users aware that they may be affected in future**.

Related party criteria

Under IAS 24 *Related party disclosures,* a related party is a person or entity that is related to the entity that is preparing its financial statements (the 'reporting entity').

Persons

IAS 24 states that a person or a close member of that person's family is related to a reporting entity if that person:

(1)   Has **control** or **joint control** over the reporting entity;

(2)   Has **significant influence** over the reporting entity; or

(3) Is a member of the **key management personnel** of the reporting entity or of a parent of the reporting entity.

Entities

An entity is related to a reporting entity if any of the following conditions applies:

(1) The entity and the reporting entity are **members of the same group** (which means that each parent, subsidiary and fellow subsidiary is related to the others).

(2) One entity is an **associate or joint venture** of the other entity (or an associate or joint venture of a member of a group of which the other entity is a member).

(3) Both entities are **joint ventures of the same third party**.

(4) One entity is a **joint venture of a third entity** and the other entity is an **associate of the third entity**.

(5) The entity is a **post-employment benefit plan** for the benefit of employees of either the reporting entity or an entity related to the reporting entity.

(6) The entity is **controlled** or **jointly controlled** by a person identified in the definition above.

(7) A person identified above as having control or joint control over the reporting entity has **significant influence** over the entity or is a member of the **key management personnel** of the entity (or of a parent of the entity).

Note that where associates and joint ventures are mentioned above, any subsidiaries of the associate or joint venture are also related to the reporting entity.

Nature of related party relationships

Within the Igbo Group

Umuofia and Mbanta are related parties of Igbo because they are **members of the same group** (both subsidiaries of Igbo). For the same reason, as fellow subsidiaries, **Umuofia and Mbanta** are also **related parties of each other**. **Mbaino is also a related party of Igbo** because it is an **associate of Igbo**. (Igbo has **significant influence** over Mbaino.)

Umuofia and Mbanta may be related parties of Mbaino. There is only one director in common and IAS 24 states that entities are not necessarily related simply because they have a director (or other member of key management personnel) in common, or because a member of key management personnel of one entity has significant influence over the other entity. However, **Mbaino is an associate of Igbo**, and therefore **a member of the group** that Umuofia and Mbanta are members of (see (2) under 'Entities' above).

Although Ikeocha was sold several months before the year end, it was a **related party of Igbo, Umuofia and Mbanta until then**. Therefore the related party relationship between Ikeocha and the Igbo group **should be disclosed** even though there were no transactions between them during the period.

Elumelu is a related party of Umuofia as a director of Umuofia controls it.

Because the director, Marvellous Ikemefuna, is not on the management board of Igbo, it is **not** clear whether Elumelu is also a related party of Igbo Group. This would depend on whether Mr Ikemefuna is considered key management personnel at a group level. Mr Ikemefuna's services as a consultant to the group may mean that a related party relationship exists. The issue would

depend on whether this role meant that he was directing or controlling a major part of the group's activities and resources.

This means that the sale of goods by Elumelu to Umuofia must be disclosed in Umuofia's individual financial statements. If Elumelu is considered to be related to Igbo Group, then the same transactions will also have to be disclosed in the group financial statements.

Between Ani and the Igbo Group

Ani is a related party of Mbanta because it exerts **significant influence** over Mbanta. This means that the **sale** of plant and equipment **to Ani must be disclosed**.

Igbo is not necessarily a related party of Ani simply because both have an investment in Mbanta. A related party relationship will only exist if one party actually **exercises influence** over another.

Between Chukwu and the Igbo Group

Chukwu is a related party of Igbo because it can exercise **significant influence** over it - this makes Igbo an associate of Chukwu. Chukwu's significant influence over Igbo gives it **significant influence over Umuofia and Mbanta** as they are controlled by Igbo and IAS 24 specifically includes subsidiaries of associates in the definition of related parties.

Mbaino is not a related party of Chukwu as Chukwu has no ability to exercise control or significant influence over Mbaino.

Disclosure of related party transactions

The main related party transactions during the year include the sale of plant and equipment by Mbanta to Ani, and the sale of goods by Elumelu to Umuofia. These are not exempt from disclosure in the group financial statements of Igbo because Ani and Elumelu are not part of the Igbo group, meaning that these are not intragroup transactions that would be cancelled on consolidation.

You proposed that disclosures should state that prices charged to related parties are set on an **arm's length basis**. This disclosure would not be strictly correct. Because the transactions took place **between related parties**, by definition it cannot have taken place on an arm's length basis. A statement that prices are charged on an arm's length basis could be seen to be **misleading**. We, as CIMA-qualified accountants, risk being in breach of IAS 24 and the principle of professional competence if we make this disclosure in the financial statements.

However, according to IAS 24, instead of saying that the 'prices are set on an arm's length basis', it is permissible to make a statement that related party transactions were 'made **on terms equivalent to those that prevail in arm's length transactions**' but only if such terms can be substantiated. Since Mbanta sold plant and equipment to Ani at **normal selling prices**, and Elumelu sold goods to Umuofia at market value, it is possible that such a statement could be made in both cases. However, we will need to ensure the terms can be substantiated.

Competency coverage

Sub-task	Technical		Business acumen		People		Leadership		Max
1	Identification of errors in goodwill working and explanation of the adjustments required	8							8
2	Explanation of the accounting treatment of the loan	6							6
3	Explanation of the reasons for disclosing related party transactions & criteria and identification of related party relationships and transactions	11							11
Total		25							25